FILENET

FileNet

A Consultant's Guide to Enterprise Content Management

Todd R. Groff and
Thomas P. Jones

LONDON AND NEW YORK

First published by Butterworth-Heinemann

This edition published 2011 by Routledge
2 Park Square, Milton Park, Abingdon, Oxon OX14 4RN
711 Third Avenue, New York, NY 10017, USA

Routledge is an imprint of the Taylor & Francis Group, an informa business

Library of Congress Cataloging-in-Publication Data
Groff, Todd R.
  FileNet: a consultant's guide to enterprise content management/
Todd R. Groff and Thomas P. Jones.—1st American pbk. ed.
    p. cm.
Includes bibliographical references and index.

  1. Information technology—Management. 2. Knowledge management.
I. Jones, Thomas P. II. Title.

  HD30.2.G758 2004
  658.4′038—dc22

ISBN - 978 0 7506 7816 2   2004000583

British Library Cataloguing-in-Publication Data
A catalogue record for this book is available from the British Library.

CONTENTS

Chapter 3

FILENET RISKS AND OPPORTUNITIES 33

Chapter 4

FILENET IMPLEMENTATION 61

Chapter 5

FILENET INTEGRATION 82

Chapter 6
FILENET ADMINISTRATION   100

Chapter 7
FILENET AND KNOWLEDGE MANAGEMENT   117

Chapter 8
FILENET AND ENTERPRISE RESOURCE
PLANNING   141

FOREWORD

In business, all things change except the quest for capital and the need for accountability. The growth objectives of a business are intricately tied to the various demands it makes for greater accountability. This book, like the authors' previous book, *Introduction to Knowledge Management—KM in Business*, looks at the key issues that cause workflow failures within organizations.

As a boy, I learned my first lessons about accountability in a battle with polio. The polio virus inflames nerves in the brain and in the spinal cord, causing paralysis of the muscles in the chest, legs, or arms. In the 1950s, contracting polio led me to dependence on artificial ventilation via the iron lung. I was told that, for the rest of my life, the iron lung would be responsible for my breathing. To the doctors, the iron lung appeared to be a miraculous solution. To me, success would mean much more than mere survival. I wanted to run, jump, and play sports; and my breathing problem was just a symptom.

Early on, I realized that although the iron lung might be responsible for the breathing that kept me alive, only I could be accountable. In other words, the duty belonged to the machine, but I would pay the price for failure. That was when I resolved to leave the iron lung behind. In those days, it was known that the only escape from the iron lung was to be "weaned" off it, one minute at a time. It was pretty scary at first, but I gradually built up my breathing strength. Eventually, I became strong enough to go from laboring through a few short minutes out of the iron lung to being able to make it on my own.

As an adult, I landed a job at Amoco's credit card billing facility in Raleigh, North Carolina. In time, I was promoted to supervisor over the Computer Operations Department, responsible for all data input and scrubbing. I quickly realized that the existing system for gas card billing suffered from massive errors, duplication of effort, and huge costs. I began investigating ways to improve the efficiency of this labor-intensive bill handling process. This was my first introduction to the need for content management technology and workflow tools.

In 1973, Amoco undertook the task of improving the efficiency of its credit card billing by introducing imaging into the process. The convenience of credit card purchases at Amoco's gasoline stations had grown Amoco's credit card billing department to 813 employees. The problem with paper is its inability to scale and its inherent mobility issues. Customers entered their personal information onto paper forms that had to be retyped as input into Amoco's computer systems. This introduced errors into the system. Because this was a common problem when integrating paper processes, Amoco began investigating imaging technologies to address the issue. The idea was that customers were unlikely to misspell their own names and addresses, and Amoco did not have to pay them to perform this data entry.

The plan was to scan signed receipts on their arrival at the processing center in Raleigh. The image would be used throughout the sales capture process; and at the end of each month, an account's images would be combined and printed in a billing statement sent to the customer.

To accomplish this, Amoco contracted to build a one-of-kind printing press to print the images of the credit card receipts at 84% of their original size (to prevent legal issues related to forgery). The 27-foot long, 11-foot high press took 63 feet of paper from end to end with a weight of 61 tons. The press printed 1200 feet per minute and microfilmed all output. In total, it cost $18 million to implement.

After the new billing process began, the business continued to grow rapidly. However, the staff providing data input support to the gas credit card business was reduced from 813 to 256 people within two years. The project completely paid for itself in the first six months of operation.

The paper-based, dual-data input, system that Amoco had previously used was a solution very similar to the iron lung that doctors used to treat my respiration problems as a child. It allowed the painful process to continue, but only with huge costs and sacrifices. For a fundamental solution, I had to create my own success.

This book deals with the complex issues surrounding enterprise content management (ECM), of which imaging is one of the oldest pieces. Improving business processes for handling paper content requires recognizing that paper-document-based processes are symptomatic solutions to larger fundamental problems. This book describes more than just FileNet's approach to ECM, it discusses many of the fundamental issues surrounding unstructured information and the managing of attention.

Fundamental solutions (like implementing content management or building up a polio survivor's lung strength) are often difficult and painful. However, relying on symptomatic solutions has two major negative side effects. First, it diverts attention away from the real problem. Second, it causes the workability of the solution to degrade over time, which reinforces the false need for more of the symptomatic solution. This cycle resembles the classic cycle of addiction in humans and the results are just as destructive.

This book on FileNet's approach to enterprise content management focuses on developing strong plans for solving fundamental business problems while improving accountability and lowering costs. I have worked with Todd and Thomas for years on some of this country's largest FileNet systems. I am confident you will find that the technical, organizational, and strategic planning information in this book provides key tools in creating your own success with your company's ECM implementation.

James E. Sparks
Business Consultant, IBM

Chapter 1

FILENET IMAGING OVERVIEW

Beware of sacrificing your adaptability on the altar of productivity, as growth must *follow* survival.

KEY POINTS

- Get an overview of enterprise content management.
- Recognize FileNet's position as a market leader in its field.
- Learn the basic setup of the FileNet organization.
- Begin to understand FileNet's architecture, strengths, and limitations.
- Understand the impact of document management strategies on overall company performance.
- Recognize FileNet's proper place in an organization's knowledge management initiative.
- Compare and contrast imaging systems with other types of electronic document management systems.

WHAT THIS BOOK IS ABOUT

This book was written to provide an independently produced, highly detailed, comprehensive overview of the FileNet company, its product

1

lines, and its role in the enterprise content management (ECM) market for large enterprises. The book details FileNet's abilities in managing attention, distributing best practices, improving feedback loops, and building a culture of knowledge sharing and innovation to facilitate continuous growth and improvement. In addition, it supplies the critical technical and organizational details required to successfully implement and support this complex, unique, and powerful system. The book also can help you avoid five key FileNet project pitfalls.

Five Common FileNet Project Pitfalls

1. Failing to understand the FileNet corporate structure before engaging in negotiations can add millions of dollars in unnecessary licensing fees to the project.
2. ECM products like FileNet function at the "points of pain" within organizations, as they require input from and education of diverse business functions such as IT, Records Management, HR, and Legal. They seek to integrate technology, people, and processes while challenging existing infrastructures and assumptions. Information hoarding on such complex projects invariably leads to unexpected costs, delayed implementation, and missed opportunities.
3. The whole concept of what a document "is" has been evolving for some time now. Our old metaphors often create more confusion than clarity. Avoiding an early effort to develop a shared language to support a shared mission increases the number of unexpressed and unidentified assumptions in a project. This substantially raises the complexity of projects.
4. The increased technical complexity created by integrating enterprise resource planning system processes with content management systems combines with the increased regulatory burden of recent legislation to create an extremely high-risk, high-profile environment for ECM project leaders, system administrators, and developers.
5. The scope and flexibility of most ECM platforms mean that merely deciding what products to buy, after you have chosen a vendor, can be extraordinarily difficult. This creates a risk of turning ECM projects into "shopping trips" that neglect the

vital analysis necessary for successfully meeting the business case objectives.

Leaders, managers, and technicians working with content management systems will find that this detailed, independent overview of FileNet can save them millions in missed opportunities and failed initiatives. The first step is to understand the meaning of *enterprise content management*. ECM systems are composed of a variety of tools, technologies, and methods that help capture, manage, store, preserve, and deliver content in support of business processes throughout an organization. In 2002, the software license revenue for the entire ECM market was $1.48 billion, which is expected to grow to $3.34 billion, a robust 22.4% compounded annual growth rate, between 2002 and 2006.

Typical ECM technology components include the following:

- *Document imaging* (DI): Software for scanning, indexing, retrieving, and archiving digital images of text, graphics, engineering drawings, and photographs. These systems usually provide workflow and limited electronic document management functionality.
- *Web content management* (WCM): Software that enables the collection, assembly, staging, maintenance, and delivery of text and graphic content primarily for disseminating information via the Web. The standard definition of WCM includes both a staging and delivery component.
- *Electronic document management* (EDM): Software that manages the complete life cycle of office documents from collaborative authoring to archiving; key features include indexing, check-in/checkout, versioning, annotations, workflow, and life cycle management.
- *Digital asset management* (DAM): Software for managing the life cycle of large collections of digital assets, such as photographic images, graphics, brand logos, and compound documents.
- *Computer output to laser disk* (COLD): Applications for storage of high-volume computer-generated reports.
- *Records management*: Applications that manage long-term document archives throughout the document life cycle.

- *Media asset management* (MAM): A subset of DAM, MAM is specific to rich media, such as video and audio, that require complex management tools.
- *Collaboration tools*: Any of several applications that promotes groups working together effectively. Typical applications include project workspaces, project management tools, automated reporting tools, and basic workflow.
- *Content integration*: Middleware that integrates multiple vendors' repositories. Also known as content federation.

Although enterprise content management encompasses all the technologies just listed, the core components required in any ECM system are document management, document imaging, web content management, records management, and workflow.

Many times, workflow is left out of lists describing ECM components; however, it is a very important feature of ECM systems. Most ECM vendors offer some type of workflow for content review and approval, but some vendors (such as FileNet and IBM) also offer production workflow for document imaging and workflow for business process management (BPM). This is important for ensuring efficient and effective data capture.

FileNet reached a very high market leadership position by focusing on active content. FileNet considers "active content" to be business objectives whose properties or behavior can launch new processes (distribute content, launch an exception routine, fire off another process to integrate with another system, and so on). FileNet has recognized the importance of having a tight relationship between active content and BPM.

FileNet's Image Services is a software product offering high-volume, digital storage, retrieval, and management of document images, transactional content, and objects of all types. Thousands of organizations worldwide have implemented FileNet systems to provide content, document, and imaging management services that are scalable, highly available, extensible, and secure. The company has come to be considered a major industry leader in the fields of imaging, document management, content management, business process management, knowledge management (KM), and business intelligence (BI). However, many have questioned whether FileNet or any other mere information management system can ever be considered KM.

Recent advances in office software technology have vastly increased the number of information/knowledge publishers, resulting in a massive increase in the amount of stored knowledge artifacts within companies. However, with the doubling of Internet traffic every 100 days and the need of most managers to deal with approximately 200 messages daily, information overload has become an obvious and terrible fact of corporate life. This shift in the information supply from scarcity to shocking abundance has taught us that the scarcest resource in the so-called information economy is attention, not ideas.

Companies have begun to ask themselves if their knowledge management efforts actually help people make better use of their limited attention or simply add more noise to the already deafening cacophony?

The KM/BI sector of the enterprise software market represents the only one to have shown any growth in 2002. Market analyst Ovum™ estimated that it will continue to be the fastest growing segment of the software market over the next five years, totaling more than $21 billion by 2006. Companies are vastly improving their knowledge management progress by building positive feedback loops into their systems. Workflow systems, like FileNet, allow business leaders to more efficiently manage the attention of their workers and increase valuable internal dialog.

However, despite an open and modular design that runs on the majority of enterprise computing platforms, FileNet's products suffer from a dearth of independently produced knowledge resources. This text has been produced to fill that information void and provide wider understanding of this complex and powerful set of products to enterprise level decision makers, project managers, and technicians. In addition, the book provides general knowledge on how to use existing document imaging and document management systems to support advanced knowledge management functions.

FileNet Company Background

The FileNet Corporation (NASDAQ: FILE) was founded by Ted Smith and specializes in multiplatform enterprise software development. Since the company's founding in 1982, FileNet's products have been implemented in 3800 organizations, including 80 of the Fortune

100. The firm's key areas of focus are business process management and enterprise content management. Recently, the company expanded its software offerings through six key strategic purchases:

■ Watermark Software, Inc. (imaging), in 1995.
■ Saros Corporation (document management) and Greenbar Software (report management/COLD), in 1996.
■ The Sequis application from Applications Partners, Inc., a FileNet ValueNet partner, in 2000.
■ eGrail, Inc., (a Web content management provider), in 2002.
■ Shana (an e-forms vendor), in 2003.

Business process management software includes products for managing the middleware IT infrastructure and corporate workflow processes. Spending in the BPM sector reached $2.26 billion in 2002, under the Aberdeen Group's calculations, with $1.7 billion of that spent on integration services. Of the three dozen or so vendors offering BPM products, IBM is the market leader, with a 16.4% share for a product portfolio that includes its IBM WebSphere MQ line. Right behind IBM is FileNet, with an 8.5% market share, and Staffware with a 7.2% share.

FileNet posted a profit of $8.3 million for the fourth quarter of 2002 and revenues rose, by 4% over the previous year, to $347 million. Additionally, Lee Roberts, FileNet chairman and CEO, commented on "overwhelmingly positive" feedback from customers regarding the FileNet P8 introduction at Insight 2003, the company's annual sales conference in Arizona.

With more and more companies realizing the importance of enabling their processes for eBusiness, the future looks bright for FileNet.

Technology Overview

FileNet Image Manager

At the heart of any FileNet document imaging solution is FileNet's Image Manager. The Image Manager (IM) product, formerly known as Image Server (IS), provides power, scalability, and performance. It is designed to deliver access to billions of unstructured objects, such as documents, faxes, e-mail, and rich media. It securely and permanently stores critical business information in a high-availability environment to protect critical content from disaster and misuse.

Using FileNet IM's integrated business process management capability, companies can respond to changing business conditions and make informed and accurate decisions.

Features and Strengths

Some benefits of Image Manager are as follows:

- Global access to critical documents and content, a Virtual File Room.
- Increased operational effectiveness and business agility.
- High level of availability and security for corporate assets.
- Prevention of critical documents and content from being unavailable due to misfiling, use by someone else, lost records, disasters, and disruptions.
- Easy integration with other systems to enhance the value of existing investments.
- Enables faster customer service, better decisions, and quicker response to rapidly changing business demands.

Image Manager was designed to bring scalability, disaster recovery, and extensive flexibility to the imaging arena. IM is a high-performance imaging solution that leverages advanced caching and a distributed architecture to manage large volumes of critical business documents and content. This increases business agility by allowing companies to provide access, within seconds, to thousands of users across multiple locations. It features components to capture, search, retrieve, and store large volumes of content including documents, faxes, e-mail, and rich media.

IM protects valuable information assets by supporting high availability, data integrity, and disaster recovery, while meeting stringent security and regulatory requirements. Since images stored on optical disks are practically unerasable, IM eases security and regulatory issues in most cases. It reduces the operating costs of managing important documents and data by eliminating lost documents. It also aids in cutting costs by using workflow to reduce the amount of time it takes to complete key business tasks and respond to new issues. Additional reductions come from integrating with existing business applications to provide simpler interfaces, better accountability, and higher job performance through more efficient sharing of critical information.

Many clients prefer FileNet solutions because the company is the recognized leader in document storage solutions utilizing WORM (write-once-read-many [times]) optical storage mediums. Although no longer the most high-tech choice for long-term fixed content document storage, WORM is a highly secure, mature, widely accepted technology. Generally, documents stored on WORM optical media are accepted just as well as the original paper documents, which may not be true of newer technologies.

Business Relationships as Document Exchanges

Most industries have a number of core processes all firms must use, due to either regulation or competitive pressures. Historically, these processes have been "document centered," centered on a document or group of documents. An example would be the way a corporate purchasing process is centered on a purchase order.

These paper-document-based processes, however, are plagued with problems such as lost and misfiled information, delays in routing, and difficulties in reporting on the status of work in process. As computers proliferated throughout corporations, many saw a potential to increase efficiency by implementing systems to support formally defined and actively monitored workflows.

In time, intelligent organizations began viewing document management implementation as far more than a simple replacement of the filing cabinet. Electronic document management strives to keep all information safe, up-to-date, and easy to find, without regard to the originating application, file type, or storage location. The goal is to ensure data integrity, reliability, availability, and security, while providing all authorized users immediate and reliable access to current information whenever and wherever needed.

By reengineering their existing paper-based systems, many companies gained the ability to track workflow, analyze new business processes, and consolidate operations. Managing documents and images is an inherent function of almost all business transactions, particularly for closed-loop processing, such as claims processing, loan applications, insurance policy underwriting, real estate transactions, and many other contractual agreements. Document management is a critical technology for producing the high-value process initiatives critical for delivering expense reduction while improving customer service and sales.

Today, many organizations struggle with the lack of accountability measures, the untracked costs and the inherent inflexibility of paper-based processes. Paper-based processes are based on highly vulnerable, fixed content that cannot be easily shared across a geographically dispersed enterprise. CEOs face the rising cost of managing large amounts of paper information in an information age. CIOs face the inability to integrate unstructured content into business processes to fully leverage the value of existing systems. Managers find they cannot accurately report to their customers, because the critical information is trapped in another stakeholder's inbox. All employees face the realities of faster business cycles and increased competition. These issues spurred corporations to attempt to eliminate paper-based processes from their businesses.

Without immediate access to the right information, knowledge workers are unable to respond quickly to internal events, external litigation, or changing customer demands. FileNet's Image Manager addresses these critical business issues, allowing for improved organizational responsiveness to customer and market demands. This has led some to regard FileNet as a potential candidate for supporting some critical enterprisewide KM activities.

Toolsets versus Out-of-the-Box Solutions

When considering any imaging product, it is very important to understand that imaging products are toolsets, not out-of-the-box solutions. Organizations must have very clear objectives with documented business processes prior to embarking on any FileNet implementation. Due to the complexity of the paper-based processes that evolved in most organizations, this will call for a considerable effort to define your terms and make sure everyone understands one another.

Document imaging and document management systems are often confused, and this confusion can lead to disastrous miscalculations.

Even though document imaging is a type of document management, document management is *not* the same as document imaging. However, DM systems often contain images and imaging systems often contain nonimaged documents. Basically, the difference between document management and imaging is more about intent than content.

Document imaging systems are designed to manage billions of pages of imaged documents, while document managers are designed to be smaller, less expensive, and more focused on *creating*, sharing, and reusing dynamic electronic documents. A DI system *captures* analog documents into digital format by scanning the previously created paper documents. This does not create editable electronic files comparable to Word documents and Web pages. Although scanned images are digital, they represent photographs of the original documents—snapshots of a moment in time.

The impact of these differences in design intent becomes apparent when you examine the way each system handles documents (see Figure 1.1). The best DI systems manage the size of the document images and break a multipage TIFF image down to a group of single-page images that appear to be one document. This enables faster retrieval of large documents across the wide area network. Most DM systems treat a TIFF image the same as any other document type, even though a 10-page TIFF image is significantly larger than a 10-page document in Microsoft Word format.

One advantage document management has over document imaging is in the cost to implement. Document management systems typically have 30–50% of the implementation cost of a document imaging system. However, if the organization is trying to manage a significantly large number of images in the DM solution, the total cost of ownership can be twice the cost of a DI system. Another issue is that DM systems are more focused on the needs of authors and DI systems are more focused on retrieval. The keys to making the right choices, as usual, are having a thorough understanding of the company's objectives and the technology.

A DM solution can be an appropriate storage system for documents the organization wants to share in a knowledge base. Help desk documents, developer notes, and bug fixes are good examples of electronic files to be stored and shared in a DM solution, because the documents captured into a DM system begin as electronic documents and keep their original form along with other versions of the

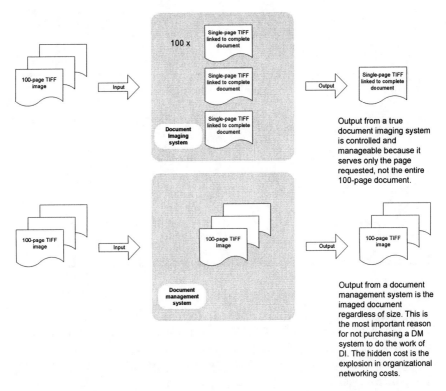

Figure 1.1
Document imaging versus document management systems

same documents. However, a document captured into an imaging system begins its life as a piece of paper, such as an invoice and must be converted to a digital format.

DM solutions may fit a niche, but they must not be seen as end-all solutions: They have limits and costs. Many departments within an organization will push for purchasing DM solutions to be used as DI solutions because of the lower advertised cost to implement DM. These departments have a narrow focus and must gain a quick return on investment (ROI). The often hidden cost to the overall organization is the undocumented rise in network infrastructure costs and the reduction in productivity for the entire networked community. Today's wide range of electronic files stretches the definition of the word *document* almost to the point of breaking.

Table 1.1

Imaging and Document Management Candidates

Good Candidates for Imaging	Good Candidates for Document Management
Records management:	**Information technology:**
Vital records management	Knowledge bases
Voter registration	Change control systems
Human resources records	Web authoring control
New accounts:	**Project management:**
Policy management	Bid management
Claims processing	Contract negotiation tools
Accounting:	**Digital archiving:**
Invoice management	Intellectual property management
Change order management	Project document libraries
Accounts payable	Decision support tools

Likewise, DI solutions are not the end-all solution either. Imaging systems do little to reduce the huge amount of document creation rework within corporations. Before an organization implements a DI solution it needs to have clearly defined expectations on ROI for imaging. Enterprise document imaging can be extremely costly, but for organizations that have high retrieval rates for paper documents, strict regulatory requirements, or a need for greater accountability, it can save millions. Table 1.1 lists some candidates for each system.

IMAGING, DOCUMENT MANAGEMENT, OR KNOWLEDGE MANAGEMENT?

Imaging systems are usually implemented to deliver one or more of the following objectives:

- Faster transactions, better workflow.
- Improved customer service.
- Meeting regulatory requirements.
- Preparing for future litigation.
- Disaster recovery.

Although both DM systems and KM systems rely on a foundation of people, processes, and technology, most KM systems are implemented to achieve the following objectives:

- Improved creativity.
- Better analysis.
- Reduced loss of experience due to attrition.
- Sharing best practices.
- Evolving procedures.
- Recognizing new opportunities.

The differences in these objectives call for a different set of planning strategies, security assumptions, and metadata requirements. While DM/DI systems empower primarily transactional functions, KM systems are much more collaborative in function and result in processes that are more circular than linear. One thing all these systems share is an emphasis on workflow automation to improve speed, accountability, and responsiveness, as well as manage workforce attention.

Too often, projects are viewed as a single trip with a reachable destination, such as the linear business process described in Figure 1.2. A fixed-scope approach is vital for preventing scope creep. However, it can also limit the learning possible during the planning and execution of a project. Following this analogy, the planners of a trip would typically get together to plan the scope of the trip. The scope would probably include planning activities such as the following:

- Define the objectives for the trip (fun, visit family, look for job, etc.).
- Choose a destination.
- Designate the time allotted for reaching destination.

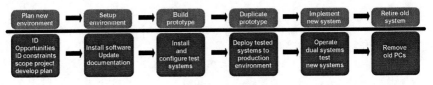

Figure 1.2
Old-style linear business process example

- Estimate the cost to reach the destination.
- Choose what mode of transportation to use.
- List any secondary destinations to visit while en route to the main destination.

Smart travelers plan their trips well. They recognize and document the components of the trip and the options and decisions agreed to during planning. The next time they plan a similar trip, the planning and execution will happen with much greater efficiency. The project may have a destination, but the way we plan and execute the project should always be evolving. Question the thoughts and conclusions that brought you to this destination. Is this the main destination or merely a resting point?

Informal and Formal Knowledge Management

All individuals perform knowledge management activities, whether they recognize it or not. Humans pass KM techniques to those within their area of influence everyday. These informal techniques are passed from parents to children, from children to other children, from children to adults, and so forth. Who taught the children in your family to always ask mom when money is the request, but ask dad when freedom is needed? The logical answer would be mom and dad. Human contact guarantees that a mixture of formal and informal KM habits and techniques evolve in any group.

An organization's activities are affected by its formal and informal KM philosophies. Often, the informal KM activities practiced within an organization conflict with its stated formal strategy. Recognizing the existence of informal and formal KM strategies is very important because it helps focus the need for practicing and improving clearly defined, formal KM practices. Formal KM activities should be an effort to correct or augment informal KM activities and better align them with the overall business objectives. Often, documents are used to formalize processes in companies. Some of the differences between formal and informal KM techniques follow.

Some informal KM activities are the following:

- Teaching a coworker to use his or her desk telephone for conferencing.

- While e-mailing a newly developed solution to a customer, sending a copy to the Help Desk so support people can solve the problem in the future.
- Adding a planning document that you have created to the departmental knowledge base so other projects can benefit from your work.
- Modeling appropriate e-mail etiquette for peers.
- Exchanging ideas and thoughts over lunch (breaking bread and breaking barriers).

Some formal KM activities are the following:

- Providing a customer service class for your department.
- Assembling a meeting to develop a new corporate value statement.
- Building a departmental knowledge base.
- Having a document you have created automatically added to the departmental knowledge base via middleware.
- Providing incentives for activities that cannot be automated.
- Blocking the users' ability to send organization-wide e-mail without a formal request.
- Using document management to reduce wasting an individual's attention.
- Using a document manager to store project information that can be used as catalyst for knowledge creation and exchange.
- Using document management as a tool for managing dialog and trust by allowing the collaboration of diverse parties to create documents while maintaining version control.
- Using document management to reduce access or control the document life cycle of confidential information.
- Using intranet banner ads to get employees to pay attention to high-quality internal authoring.

FileNet allows formalizing some KM activities, mostly through the workflow. FileNet is not KM in itself but a component of and used in many KM activities. For example, a car dealer's repair invoice could be managed through FileNet's workflow to monitor repetitive issues and report the issues and solutions to the car manufacture's design team, eventually be disseminated to the assembly line to reduce defects, and the future need for dealer repairs.

KM Initiatives and Activities

FileNet creates products used in activities belonging to strategic initiatives. The confusion surrounding whether or not information management is a part of knowledge management is rooted in the continual loud statements of what KM is not and the quiet whispers of what it might be. Information management may not be knowledge management, but it is definitely used in knowledge management activities and initiatives.

Initiatives are high-level strategies started, typically at the top of a department or organization, to set a direction and create a shared vision. If not properly planned, initiatives may lack depth of description and real strategy. A real initiative has measurable activities and deliverables (the tactical component of the overall strategy). An initiative that lacks real activities and deliverables may require the implementation team to flesh out the details.

For example, the following initiatives lack a depth of description:

- Knowledge management.
- Focus on core competencies.
- Improved efficiency.
- World-class customer service.

Real initiatives, however, have specific details:

- Knowledge management—Improve our internal collaboration by improving employees access to collaboration tools such as document management, e-mail, teleconferencing, and video conferencing.
- Focus on core competencies—Use workflow tools to automate processes and improve accountability within our core business processes.
- Improved efficiency—Remove paper from the accounts payables process.
- Better customer service—Implement change control, bullet-proof e-mail, and provide 99.9% system uptime standards.

Many products offered by companies are not solely knowledge management products but are used in activities that support KM initiatives. In a nutshell, it is our belief that the need for using KM within existing projects is greater than for creating independent knowledge management projects. Critical KM concepts such as increasing feedback and dialog while maximizing the user's attention and effectiveness should be goals of all projects not just KM projects.

What Defines a KM System?

A KM system utilizes people, processes, and technology to provide content management, searching, collaboration, and learning to employees. This is addressed in more detail as the book progresses. For now, remember the three key enablers of KM (people, processes, and technology) and the four key components of KM (content management, searching, collaboration, and learning). Content within your FileNet system may serve traditional document imaging/document management roles or the same content may serve KM goals. The difference is usually in the context, objectives, and the workflow.

Most experts agree that any KM system that does not address all four key components represents a less-than-complete solution. Additionally, if it does not address the people, processes, and technologies, it is no solution at all. Unfortunately, showing hard dollars for ROI from KM systems is extremely difficult. To some consultants, this rules out KM implementations for any but the largest, wealthiest companies. The solution to this problem may be in seeking KM objectives in the context of more accepted system implementations that can provide clearer ROI numbers. We talk more about this in later chapters.

SUCCESS STORY

A nearly 100-year-old insurance company decided that it was losing competitive advantage by being too slow in issuing new insurance policies. A paper-based system requiring documents to flow from the agencies to the central office created excessive delays in approving policies. The company needed an automated Web-based system that could issue a policy with very limited human intervention. The project would require prospects and agents to access and complete forms online. The system would then interface with motor vehicle records, credit rating agencies, and the company's internal systems.

The online system would also need to handle exceptions and be deployed quickly.

The solution that FileNet delivered included their Claims Processing module, an ECM solution developed specifically for the property and casualty insurance industry. Running on a Microsoft Windows 2000 Web server, the FileNet Insurance Claims Processing application automatically flags exceptions and routes them to the appropriate underwriter based on the prospect's location and other criteria. Distribution functions and built-in routing and matching of data to files were customized for the specific business process needs. FileNet's ECM and workflow solution enabled the insurance company to successfully accomplish the following business objectives:

- Automate the issuance of quotes and policies to reduce processing time from seven days to a matter of minutes.
- Alleviate the bottlenecks from exceptions that require a more intensive, tailored underwriting review.
- Reduce data entry errors by having the customer enter his or her own information.
- Increase customer satisfaction by providing faster responses to new policy requests.

Chapter 2

FILENET PRODUCTS AND SERVICES

Computers are incredibly fast, accurate, and stupid. Human beings are incredibly slow, inaccurate, and brilliant. Together they are powerful beyond imagination.

Albert Einstein (1879–1955)

KEY OBJECTIVES

■ Awareness of the key divisions within FileNet and how they interact with one another.

■ Knowledge of which divisions within FileNet support particular technologies and who to contact with questions and other issues.

■ Understanding of FileNet's inherent recovery capabilities as well as options for supporting higher levels of disaster recovery.

■ Awareness of the training and certification opportunities FileNet offers and how to stay up-to-date on the platform.

The Company behind the Curtain

One could be awestruck by the size and complexity of the Mighty Oz—until the curtain is pulled aside. In the same way, dealing with the FileNet Corporation can be intimidating, if you do not understand its organizational structure. This chapter discusses FileNet's products and the use of those products as components of knowledge and content management, but what use is this information if you are unable to gain access to bids, estimates, and proposals for FileNet products and services?

A difficulty in managing information technology (IT) resources is knowing when to train for expertise and when to train for project management. IT resources are not cheap to own and often spread very thin over multiple initiatives. Because of the need to operate IT departments at lower costs, many organizations look offshore to outsource much of their IT infrastructure. The issue with this practice is recovering the cost to move the jobs overseas, while maintaining the same level of competence.

These complexities can be simplified by using FileNet resources through a multitude of FileNet avenues. Figure 2.1 shows many areas of an IT department's responsibilities and the following paragraphs examine the relationship between these functions and the various groups within FileNet.

IT Departmental Responsibilities

- *Projects affecting infrastructure and responsibilities.* New projects increase the IT department's responsibility by adding information, equipment, and users. The project itself requires resources to compete and resources are required on a continual basis to administrate the project.
- *Upgrading the existing infrastructure.* Often, the ability to keep a system operating and current, on the application level, depends on earlier project management efforts and similar projects that put new systems in place.
- *Maintaining technical training.* Most IT departments have established efforts to maintain a level of technical expertise within a department. Often, performance metrics are tied to industry certification.

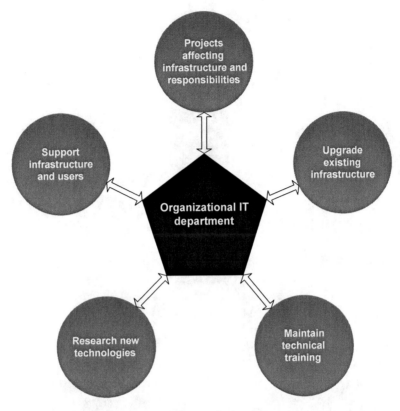

Figure 2.1
Organizational Information Technology responsibilities

■ *Researching new technologies.* IT departments are continually challenged to bring technology to bear on organizational issues. To accomplish this, a certain amount of time must be spent researching new technologies.

■ *Supporting infrastructure and users.* This represents the normal administration function performed by IT departments to ensure that existing systems are maintained and end user issues are handled. One area often overlooked by IT departments is the use of outsourcing on a smaller, more-limited scale. FileNet offers many services that can be purchased to offset the need for IT departments to maintain significant redundancy in their groups. Figure 2.2 shows how FileNet's internal and

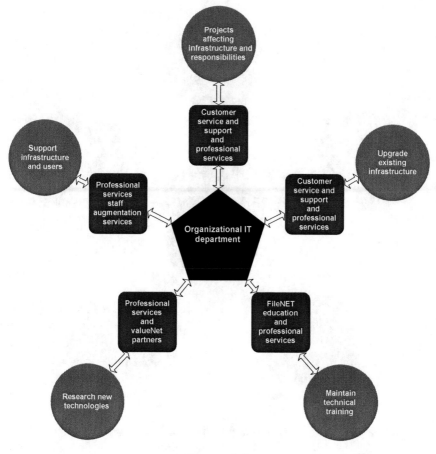

Figure 2.2
Organizational Information Technology responsibilities with FileNet's help

external groups are structured to support the IT Department's responsibilities.

Divisions and the Functions They Support

■ *Projects affecting infrastructure and responsibilities.* New projects constitute an excellent area to use FileNet resources. FileNet requires that systems be installed and upgraded by certified FileNet engineers. The cost to maintain these resources internally can be prohibitive to many organizations. By farming out this work to FileNet or a ValueNet® partner, an organization's IT department can oversee the work without having to train staff members to actually do the work.

- *Upgrading the existing infrastructure.* Major system upgrades also must be performed by a certified FileNet engineer, which makes this another area in which to use a FileNet or ValueNet resource. During upgrades, the installation of the FileNet software is handled by Customer Service and Support (CS&S); however, data migration or Oracle/database work is typically handled by FileNet's Professional Services (PS).

- *Maintaining technical training.* FileNet offers many educational programs for certification, including administrator, developer, technician, and other programs for ValueNet partners. One option for education that is not often discussed is using a department's education dollars to bring CS&S and PS engineers on-site to review configurations and advise the support team on ways to improve stability, performance, and functionality. This time can be purchased in blocks and used in place of certification training, which typically focuses on a broad range of skills. The training can be tailored to focus on the specific environment being supported.

- *Researching new technologies.* Similar to the preceding, research can utilize CS&S or PS engineers to focus on what is changing at FileNet and how it could be tailored to the specific IT environment. Another resource that can be used in this area of interest that will cost the organization only time is bringing in a FileNet-certified salesperson.

- *Supporting the infrastructure and users.* Often IT groups supporting FileNet are lean. This can be an issue when handling extended illnesses or just covering vacations. FileNet Professional Services can help with "staff augmentation services."

FILENET VALUENET PARTNERS AND CUSTOMER SERVICE AND SUPPORT

FileNet markets its products and services in more than 90 countries through its own global sales, support organizations, professional services, and ValueNet partners. The ValueNet partners reach areas of the world that, in some cases, are without a FileNet corporate presence. This program is made up of value-added resellers (VARs), system integrators, consultants, independent software vendors, and service providers. There are well over 500 of these partners worldwide, with only half that number in the United States. This network of partners increases the product and service options for FileNet customers. The ValueNet partners also offer valuable resources for knowledge exchange and feedback from independent companies that possess some of the most knowledgeable individuals in the content management world.

FileNet Sales

One of the most difficult areas of FileNet to understand is the sales organization. The difficulty arises not from their organizational structure but from the seeming lack of pricing structure. The sales team is knowledgeable about the company's product lines but, like most sales organizations, it tends to recommend as much software as possible. Make a point of knowing what type of engineer you are speaking to whenever dealing with FileNet engineers, this is because many are "sales engineers."

For FileNet VARs and other official partners, the company offers promotional materials via the FileNet eXtra site. The website provides easy access to a wealth of sales resources to help them sell FileNet solutions, as well as answer customer questions abut competing products. The FileNet eXtra website is at www.FileNet.com/eXtra/.

FileNet Customer Service and Support

When an organization purchases a FileNet system with a support agreement, the support is provided by the company's Customer Service and Support Department. Installations, upgrades, and issues go through CS&S support by either phone or e-mail. Through FileNet's Customer Service and Support website, it is possible to open and monitor cases, retrieve resources such as software patch updates, product documentation, or query FileNet's knowledge base 24 hours a day. To use the online CS&S system an organization must contact its salesperson for authorization to get a logon name and password. The FileNet CS&S website is at www.css.FileNet.com/.

Professional Services

FileNet Professional Services is a key component when planning and implementing any optimization or enhancement to your FileNet solution. Because of the scarcity of FileNet published information, few know more about the capabilities of this product line than the FileNet Professional Services Department. PS breaks down into the following areas: consulting services, implementation services, and system enhancement services.

Consulting Services

The consulting services branch of Professional Services focuses on content and process challenges and reaching strategic goals. Consulting services also focuses on improving efficiency through applied technology. It also helps companies define their business needs. The components of consulting services are application performance services, capture express services, mentoring services, solution services, and staff augmentation services.

Consulting services' application performance services provides key functionality in using Compuware® application performance tools to provide quantified analysis reports, especially by identifying specific performance problems that may arise during production rollout to allow for proactive corrective action to enhance user acceptance of the application.

FileNet's capture express component has powerful functionality, but implementation can be difficult because of its quirky nature. The product is one of the company's least refined and can be a challenge to implement, especially over a wide area network (WAN). The document capture process provides the foundation for any imaging system, and it is crucial that your firm's needs be clearly defined from the beginning of the imaging system project. Capture express services provides a suite of software tools that enhances FileNet capture's functionality.

Finding well-trained staff for FileNet positions within a company can be difficult and having extra project staff can be cost prohibitive. FileNet recognizes this profit opportunity and offers professional services staff for organizations to provide them FileNet-centered expertise and assistance within following areas:

■ Project management.
■ Custom application design and development.
■ Quality assurance.
■ System administration.
■ Enterprise network and interface issues.
■ Application rollout assistance.

The difficulty in working with FileNet PS on projects is gaining an estimate (Class C, ±30%) of cost before the detailed project planning begins. Similar to the chicken or egg analogy, FileNet typically cannot give reasonable estimates based on only a high-level project scope and plan. This, however, is not that unusual in the consulting field.

Implementation Services

To meet certification requirements and ensure the quality of implementations, FileNet Implementation Services is available. Remember, FileNet products are toolsets that require tailoring to individual company goals, systems, and processes. The technology is adaptable, but with the adaptability comes complexity of implementation.

The implementation services offered include installation packages and launch services.

FileNet offers fixed-fee package services to cover a variety of installations and learning services. These services are vital to maintain the organization's FileNet system certification. Each FileNet enterprise content management suite has an associated installation package. *Caution*: Travel and expenses are often not included in the initial bids.

FileNet offers services under the umbrella of launch services, typically a catchall area that basically means purchasing blocks of hours. The statements of work that are joined to these blocks are generic and designed to protect FileNet from being required to deliver anything substantial. To ensure its project's success, an organization should insist on interviewing the FileNet engineer assigned to execute the block of hours prior to signing off on the statement of work. The interview process is used to verify that the person FileNet recommends has the skill set needed.

System Enhancement Services

Finding high-quality FileNet resources can be a serious issue: System Enhancement Services fills the gap between owning administrative resources and true enhancement/project resources. The FileNet product line is complex and the constant renaming of products and services adds to the confusion with that product line. Expect to need FileNet's help to make any major changes or upgrades to your system. The services offered include enhanced availability services, image conversion services, media migration services, platform conversion services, and utility software solutions.

The enhanced availability services group of FileNet specialists guide an organization in designing and building a customized solution for high availability. These solutions typically include disaster recovery services for protection from a natural disaster and multisystem synchronization (MSS) for replicating multiple systems data to other domains. It is usually a good idea to pursue high availability, if you are already working on disaster recovery. The additional costs are not that high, and they allow the users to see immediate benefit from implementing a disaster recovery system that (ideally) may not ever be needed.

Imaging systems typically are built to capture images but not to easily give up those images. FileNet, along with most image companies, does not assist customers with leaving their platform. If you are moving from a non-FileNet platform to FileNet, FileNet's image conversion services typically provides resources to smooth the cutover.

Migrating data from FileNet's proprietary systems and hardware can be challenging. If an organization does not own FileNet resources that already have migrated FileNet system data, it would be advisable to contract FileNet's image conversion services. Although these services are relatively expensive, the data typically are irreplaceable.

Simply moving from one media format (such as 12 GB optical platters) to another (like magnetic storage or 30 GB optical platters) can be difficult in systems of high complexity and multiple integration points. Media migration services offer many scripts to mitigate the difficulties inherent in FileNet media migration.

Similar to the other conversion services offered, FileNet has defined processes and service offerings for migrating between hardware platforms and different operating systems. Platform conversion services support conversions between supported platforms including Sun, Hewlett-Packard, IBM, and Microsoft NT platforms and Oracle, Sybase, and SQL databases.

As with most imaging applications, FileNet systems require specialized utility tools to help organizations take advantage of the inherent architecture and design of the FileNet environment. FileNet provides utilities, such as DART and HPII/MRII, for automated batch image imports and automated backup of optical images. If you believe that the utility your organization needs is fairly common, it may be already developed and available from FileNet's utility software solutions group.

Disaster Recovery Hot-Site Services

FileNet can provide a comprehensive solution for system recoverability for an organization's mission-critical document management applications. Effective disaster recovery services offer the option of not investing in redundant document management systems or risk losing business as a result of an unplanned service interruption.

A "hot-site" disaster recovery facility contains duplicate computers and equipment that an organization can use to immediately replace a system lost in a disaster. FileNet is partnered with Comdisco Inc., a recognized leader in business continuity services, to provide a complete hot-site disaster recovery solution. The partnership offers a disaster recovery hot-site service designed to recover all FileNet document management environment in 24 hours or less following a disaster.

The hot-site hardware configurations include Image Manager (Image Services) and content services servers, optical systems, and facsimile server hardware, which support all the operating system platforms currently available for FileNet software. Organizations subscribing to the service can access the system directly through a variety of network access configurations including T1 connections and Sonnet-Ring capability.

Testing and availability features of this service include dedicated access to these systems available 24/7 in the event of a disaster and schedulable hours each year for testing the system's recovery capacities validity and integrity.

In case the disaster reduces an organization's technical team or the organization is new to this type of implementation, full-time, dedicated, on-site FileNet technical resources are available to provide restoration and network connectivity expertise when conducting restoration testing or during an actual disaster recovery effort. This means you can leverage the technical skills and experience of both FileNet Professional Services and Comdisco Inc. to augment your recovery skill set.

For disasters that disable complete sites including facilities, this partnership includes work area recovery facilities in all major metropolitan locations. These facilities include office space, voice capability, and a variety of office equipment such as PCs, printers, fax machines, and desktop scanners. In areas where these facilities are unavailable, the partnership offers mobile recovery units.

This service binds FileNet Professional Services to assuming responsibility for restoration of an organization's system, the FileNet integrated document management environment, and databases. Comdisco Inc. technical support personnel assume responsibility for the establishment and maintenance of the network backup capability as well as all logistical and facility issues.

The dedicated on-site FileNet Professional Services disaster recovery consulting specialist and the disaster recovery program manager provide all necessary technical and operational support during disaster recovery testing exercises as well as during an actual recovery. The disaster recovery program manager can also provide assistance in the development of an organization's disaster recovery objectives.

The same FileNet Customer Service and Support personnel, responsible for normal system support assistance assume responsibility for the restoration and recovery of an organization's environment at the client-side recovery facility. This support is provided regardless of whether the client chose to use the nearest Comdisco Inc. work area recovery facility or a facility internal to the organization.

FileNet Education

FileNet's 26 training locations around the world provide training for its customers and partners. Distance learning options, including online training and virtual classrooms, are also available. Training classes are conducted at FileNet's Costa Mesa, California, headquarters; its regional education centers; and FileNet-authorized education partner locations around the world. FileNet certified professional status is given to professionals that pass the required series of online exams.

FileNet offers five levels of certification that constitute several tracks to train consultants, support personnel, development personnel, and administration personnel for FileNet's extensive product line. Each certification track consists of around 15 classes, costing around $2800. The certification year runs from April 16 to April 15. The purpose of the certification year is to establish which individuals and organizations maintain the most up-to-date certification status. To maintain current certification, an individual must complete the new requirements for the current certification year by the given deadline. One who is 2003 certified must achieve the 2004 certification requirements by April 15, 2004.

FileNet education locations include the following:

- Costa Mesa, California.
- Atlanta, Georgia.
- Nr Basingstoke, Hampshire, United Kingdom.
- Amstelveen, The Netherlands.
- Hamburg, Germany.
- Paris, France.
- Madrid, Spain.
- Rome, Italy.
- Sydney, Australia.

FileNet Certification

The FileNet certification program also drives revenue into the company. Typically, maintenance contracts insist on the use of FileNet certified personnel for major system changes. This, combined with a general lack of independent information relating to FileNet, makes it a near certainty that a client will hire professionals from FileNet's Customer Support and Professional Services.

This might lead you to discount the need for training your own personnel, since so much work has to be done by FileNet employees. However, knowledgeable, well-trained internal FileNet support technicians are often your best defense against being "taken to the cleaners" by FileNet's extremely aggressive sales force.

The best way to stay up-to-date on FileNet's educational offerings is to watch the FCP bulletins and the Global Learning Services website at www.FileNet.com/English/Services_&_Support/Global_Learning_Services/Certification_Programs/

Naming Conventions

One of the most difficult issues in working with FileNet is the endless renaming of products and services. For example, the FileNet product for sharing IS services across extended locations has been called Distributive Image Services (DIS), Remote Image Server (RIS), Batch Entry Services (BES), and Remote Application Server (RAS). Establishing and maintaining clearly defined terminology throughout a project is a vital component of a successful FileNet implementation.

Sending imaging and document management support personnel for training from FileNet's Global Learning Services is a great way to get your team speaking the same language. Ramping up your employees' knowledge of this critical enterprise system provides significant protection against an overeager FileNet sales force as well as numerous money-saving opportunities. In the next chapter, we explore more ways to limit risks and increase opportunities using FileNet's advanced content management capabilities.

Success Story

After growing through acquisitions, an organization's private client services (PCS) group had to deal with a wide range of beneficiary trust content management systems. Decision making was being adversely affected by the need for customer service representatives to spend two-thirds of their time tracking down information. It was determined that a single intranet solution was needed for managers, and the organization was challenged with implementing an ECM solution.

Using eProcess Services and Content Services, FileNet linked the trust offices and Web-enabled key administrative transactions. By automating the PCS group's paper-based processes, trust administrators now can access the clients' files online. When complete, the information is forwarded to the trust officer, who reviews the content and renders a decision. If approved, the system automatically transfers the funds.

This solution enabled the organization to accomplish the following:

■ Greatly reduce the time required to make a decision on payment requests from three or more days to one.
■ Improve customer service through increased performance by the trust administrators.
■ Provide online access to each trust application to support problem solving and create a clear audit trail.
■ Focus more resources on building new revenue streams and less to administrative tasks.

Chapter 3

FileNet Risks and Opportunities

Forty percent of enterprises that experience a disaster will go out of business within five years. In some cases, the disruption to business operations causes customers to lose confidence in the organization's viability. In other cases, the cost of recovery is simply too great.

—Aftermath: Disaster Recovery, Gartner Research,
September 2001

Key Objectives

- Explore some of the ways FileNet can ease the growing pains of organizations in the midst of massive changes resulting from mergers and acquisitions.
- Become familiar with the Sarbanes-Oxley Act of 2002 and learn what content management, data integrity, process management, and security improvements enterprises need to be in compliance.
- Understand the need for clearly defined data ownership roles and document retention policies before any system implementation.
- Realize the advantages and disadvantages of the various storage mediums and strategies FileNet offers.

33

- Learn how to set up a distributed data capture center as well as the opportunities and risks of decentralized capture operations.
- Understand features and options for FileNet's standard disaster recovery and business continuance strategies.
- Learn the key factors in determining the return on investment of imaging paper documents for bidding a FileNet implementation.
- Understand content management's impact on attention and trust within organizations.
- Learn how to use FileNet to properly integrate records retention and content management for maximum efficiency and regulatory compliance.
- Understand the competing objectives that must be balanced when organizing unstructured data and establishing document life cycles.
- Know the relationship between document families and document classes within a FileNet system.

Organizational Change

Mergers, acquisitions, and divestments create some of the thorniest issues of change management a company is likely to experience. Looking on the bright side, these changes also provide unique opportunities to realize the value of your company's FileNet investment. In this section, we illustrate some of the ways FileNet eases the growing pains of organizations in the midst of massive change.

Trust is an extremely valuable commodity in any relationship, and trust is in especially short supply during mergers. Digitized records reduce the purchasing company's worry of acquisition targets shredding valuable information. Companies maintaining electronic repositories of corporate information that are indexed by powerful databases and stored on WORM optical platters have demonstrated an effort to value their information and their employee's attention.

Although the vital tacit knowledge that lives in the minds of the workers is very difficult to capture, bulk scanning of documents provides a way to quickly capture a large amount of the most critical business information. Once the documents have been captured digitally, teams rather than individuals can do the analysis without document-sharing conflicts.

Successful mergers and acquisitions depend on a number of key factors. Two key factors FileNet can help with are information sharing and managing accountabilities. In any transition, a large number of constituents need to receive not only initial information but also a continuing flow of information as the transition evolves. Obviously, key constituents include customers, suppliers, and employees. However, the transition group often extends to include members of the media, attorneys, accountants, and consultants.

Sadly, according to studies by Harvard University and the American Management Association, the majority of mergers and acquisitions do not create wealth for the acquiring companies' shareholders. To make these transitions smoother, considerable foresight, planning, and execution skill are involved.

The first step in an acquisition is the due diligence phase. In this phase, a huge amount of various documents must be assembled and distributed effectively. These items include balance sheets and other financial documents, management structure documentation, marketing reports, process mappings, project feasibility studies, HR policies, and a mountain of other documents. Careful scrutiny of legal documents during the due diligence phase typically calls for this initial analysis to be conducted by a team of legal experts.

The complexities of merger issues require a disciplined approach, if the transition is to go well. To quickly establish a collaborative relationship between the two organizations, insist on a well-planned and sustained change management process. Document management technology allows building automatic escalation processes into the workflow. This helps to ensure clear communications, easy to follow paper trails, and strong accountability—for an orderly transition.

Achieving significant reductions in prime storage space through elimination of filing cabinets is also important during a merger. Just about every transaction in which a business participates results in a new document being created. Over time, these massive piles of paper become a drag on the speed, efficiency, and customer service quality of any business. However, there are more reasons to move away from paper-based processes than cost savings alone.

The Sarbanes-Oxley Act of 2002 provides penalties of up to 20 years imprisonment for corporate executives found guilty of destroying, altering, or fabricating records in federal investigations or schemes to defraud investors or for filing false financial statements with the SEC. Similarly, the Health Insurance Portability and Accountability Act (HIPAA) of 1996 and the Gramm-Leach-Bliley Act (GLBA) of 1999 may hold public companies accountable for controlling the security of and access to a wide range of personally identifiable information.

The Sarbanes-Oxley Act of 2002

Good records management depends on both business processes and technology. Smart purchasing and planning decisions can lead to transparent systems that add sufficient accountability to end the trend of massive corporate scandals. The need for strengthening finance, accounting, and document management processes, in the light of Enron, WorldCom, and the Sarbanes-Oxley Act of 2002, is now obvious. This provides an excellent opportunity to pursue much needed data integrity, integration, and security improvements. Enterprises with previously implemented content management and workflow systems have a clear advantage in winning the credibility to be gained from early adoption of these reforms.

The Sarbanes-Oxley Act of 2002 creates two new crimes that penalize corruptly altering, destroying, mutilating, or concealing documents and impose a responsibility to preserve certain litigation-related documents. This means that CIOs can be held personally responsible for bad financial data. Whether or not CIOs make the types of accounting decisions whose ethics can be questioned, they are certainly building the systems whose data are relied on to make those decisions. If these systems are discovered to have provided inaccurate data, the senior management may be forced to pay a terrible price.

Start thinking now about the process controls within your company. Can you document and explain the financial processes that make up your financial reports? Have these processes been mapped? Are they being accurately monitored? Are they evolving to meet the regulatory constraints that have been recently imposed? Automated process metrics and workflow mapping will be critical to all publicly funded companies hoping to meet the requirements of this new round of financial management reform.

Key Sarbanes-Oxley Sections Relating to Records and Process Management

- According to Section 103, firms must prepare and maintain audit work papers that support the auditor's conclusions for seven years.
- Section 105 explores investigation and disciplinary proceedings with regard to the use of documents.
- Section 302 mandates generating up-to-date, accurate reports on internal controls and financial statements that CEOs and CFOs can sign.
- Section 404 examines changes to annual reports to include an internal control report that shows the procedures and structure of financial reporting as well as an assessment of their effectiveness.
- Section 802 amends parts of the U.S. Code relating to records management, making it pertain to private companies in addition to those publicly traded.
- Section 1102 describes penalties for tampering with a critical record or otherwise impeding a compliance investigation.
- Section 1520 defines rules for retention of audit documents and audit review papers.
- Titles 8 and 11 of the act make it a felony to "knowingly" destroy or create documents to "impede, obstruct or influence" any existing or contemplated federal investigation.

Corporate finance officers now are required to view and confirm the effectiveness of all financially related business processes. Otherwise, they cannot ensure that the numbers from the company's financial information systems are "true and accurate." Other parts of the act direct corporations to electronically file public disclosures and to post statements "on a publicly accessible Internet site not later than the end of the business day following that filing." This may indicate a need for considering Web content management solutions within some organizations.

The Health Insurance Portability and Accountability Act of 1996

The first-ever federal privacy standards to protect every patient's medical records and other health information provided to health plans, doctors, hospitals, and other health care providers took effect on April 14, 2003. Developed by the Department of Health and Human Services (HHS), these new standards provide patients access to their medical records and more control over how their personal health information is used and disclosed. They represent a uniform, federal floor of privacy protection for consumers across the country. State laws providing additional protection to consumers are not affected by this new rule.

Congress called on HHS to issue patient privacy protections as part of the Health Insurance Portability and Accountability Act of 1996. HIPAA includes provisions designed to encourage electronic transactions and also requires new safeguards to protect the security and confidentiality of health information. The final regulation covers health plans, health care clearinghouses, and those health care providers that conduct certain financial and administrative transactions (e.g., enrollment, billing, and eligibility verification) electronically. Most health insurers, pharmacies, doctors, and other health care providers are required to comply with these federal standards beginning April 14, 2003. As provided by Congress, certain small health plans had an additional year to comply. The HIPAA regulations protect medical records and other individually identifiable health information, whether on paper, in computers, or communicated orally.

HIPAA Civil and Criminal Penalties

Congress provides civil and criminal penalties for covered entities that misuse personal health information. For civil violations of the standards, the Department of Health and Human Services' Office for Civil Rights may impose monetary penalties of up to $100 per violation, up to $25,000 per year, for each requirement or prohibition violated. Criminal penalties apply for certain actions, such as knowingly obtaining protected health information in violation of the law. Criminal penalties can range up to $50,000 and one year in prison for certain offenses, up to $100,000 and up to five years in prison if the offenses are committed under "false pretenses," and up to $250,000 and up to 10 years in prison if the offenses are committed with the intent to sell, transfer, or use protected health information for commercial advantage, personal gain, or malicious harm.

Many organizations are now leveraging a new solution from FileNet and Steelpoint. The compliance and litigation risk management (CLRM) solution utilizes enterprise content management products from FileNet and an eDiscovery and litigation support applications from Steelpoint. It manages the paper-based and electronically stored data within an organization, including claims, policies, rules, and the like, to locate problem areas and uses workflow technology to drive the correct mitigation action in a rapid, efficient, and effective manner.

Increasing adoption of digital technologies, when combined with such initiatives as the Sarbanes-Oxley Act and HIPAA, change the rules for content management within many types of organizations. Obsolete information handling rules and procedures need to be updated to be in compliance with the act. HIPAA's security and privacy regulations require both access control (so that only the right individuals can obtain medical records) and distribution auditing (so that institutions can account for every person looking at medical records). Companies like IBM and FileNet, which market enterprise-grade document imaging systems, are well positioned to benefit from the need to satisfy HIPAA requirements.

Informational Responsibilities

One of the best ways to reduce the amount of risk in FileNet projects is to clearly establish and maintain data ownership roles. When companies establish FileNet libraries, they almost always make it very clear who has the *responsibility* for keeping the system alive and functional. Unfortunately, it is rare for companies to make it clear who has *authority* over the data. Clearly defined data ownership roles for the business users will become increasingly important (and difficult to identify) as the system ages.

An important aspect of data ownership is setting up a retention policy. It is vital that the document retention period be determined while the project is being planned. During project planning, the information is fresh and the stakeholders already have a commitment to the success of the project. If you wait until you run out of space on your system to make decisions on what you can delete and what you must keep, you are bound to have problems. Expect to find few volunteers for deciding what must be kept and what is free to be purged. The risk to reward ratio for this type of work is not very appealing to most executives.

Retention is just as relevant when discussing electronic information as when discussing paper-stored information, because the stakes are very high. It is vital to define the retention period for electronic information and define the responsibility and process for removing the information as it reaches its retention date.

One limitation to optical storage/WORM (Write Once Read Many) media is the difficulty in destroying the information that has reached its end of life. This is ironic since such "limitation" was the key benefit WORM technology was implemented to provide. WORM technology attempts to prevent items from ever being lost. In this age of massive litigation, prevention of document loss is definitely a two-edged sword. I say that it *attempts* to prevent items from being lost, because it is not always wholly successful.

The technology used for consumer music CDs is one application of WORM technology. Anyone who has been around long enough to see the transition from vinyl albums to CDs has observed some data loss from WORM media. CDs are far from indestructible, and although they may not lose audio quality as easily, an errant fingerprint can cause playback problems that are at least as significant as scratches on records.

Data owners need training to develop the necessary business knowledge to make good judgments about tricky issues like retention priorities, bulk exports, data purges, and evolving access rules. Large organizations may look for this training to be provided by internal teams assembled from such departments as IT, Legal, and Records Management or consider outsourcing this training.

Any time a new document management project is begun, the data owners should insist on the inclusion of a strategy for exporting all the data out of the new system in a widely compatible format. This is the type of work XML was created to do. A well-thought-out exit strategy reduces future project costs and improves the final ROI of those projects, by building in bulk import and export functionality. This is also important from a data mobility standpoint. The ability to export selective batches of documents to CD media can cut costs substantially when large numbers of documents must be exported for a third party. Sometimes this capability can even provide a new revenue source.

With any large document management system, the need eventually arises for mass import and export operations, often due to mergers, litigation, audits, or regulatory compliance issues. A good rule of thumb is to never put critical organizational information into any system without having a tested exit strategy. It seems counterintuitive to go into a new implementation focusing on obsolescence and disasters, but this is why skyscrapers are not built with only one fire exit.

OPTICAL VERSUS MAGNETIC STORAGE

When architecting a content management system, what type of storage should be purchased? This is a critical question that the system's disaster recovery capabilities, maintenance costs, and retrieval performance all depend on. FileNet offers two main options: OSAR (optical storage and retrieval) and MSAR (magnetic storage and retrieval). FileNet's optical technology is a very secure, solid option for the long-term storage of organizational documents. However, one of the leaders in the field of data storage, EMC, has recently released its Centera® product, which offers a cutting-edge storage area network (SAN) solution with some extremely advanced features for data validity checking, high availability, and disaster recovery.

The physical platters in a FileNet OSAR have a 70-year expected life; however, an optical reader that supports drivers for available server equipment would be needed, 70 years hence, to read the old media. Since software manufacturers have embraced the policy of not supporting obsolete products and hardware manufacturers quickly stop producing obsolete hardware, the possibility is real that, in 70 years or so, old media may be unreadable on existing technology. This brings up the important issue of company viability.

When discussing content management, document management, and imaging repositories, the two biggest players are FileNet and IBM. Both companies have shown a commitment to content, document, and imaging repositories. IBM's strength is in being the larger of the two companies, and FileNet's strength is that it specializes in content management systems. Although either company may eventually decide the get out of the document management market, FileNet has few other choices, since managing documents has always been the whole pie for them.

Centralized versus Decentralized Capture

Capture is the process of adding content to a repository, whether an electronic document, a paper document and image, a piece of code, or something else. Most electronic document management systems use a decentralized capture method that allows a user to add content from the same client software used to search and view existing content.

Organizations with imaging management systems often struggle with deciding whether to use centralized or decentralized document capture. This is because scanning requires specialized equipment and the images are typically not keyword searchable, so they require detailed indexing.

The need for uniform indexing procedures and the cost of scanning equipment typically are the driving factors for companies to adopt centralized capture (Figure 3.1). Also, global organizations or outsourcing providers sometimes use imaging to bypass certain postal regulations that often prevent financial documents from leaving their country of origin. These regulations, along with the cost of domestic and foreign labor, often cause organizations to consider developing a decentralized capture system (Figure 3.2).

Decentralized document capture clients require access to the main image system repository and can face challenges such as network bandwidth, firewall rules, domain name services (DNS) issues, language, hardware export restrictions, overseas software licensing, time zone conflicts, hardware power requirements, change control, and secure data center facilities. Also, the goal of saving millions by eliminating centralized data capture operations often proves quite elusive. Many organizations belatedly realize that they have moved performance of the data capture task away from relatively low-wage clerical workers and toward much higher-wage employees.

FileNet and its partners have developed many products to support both centralized and decentralized capture within organizations. The

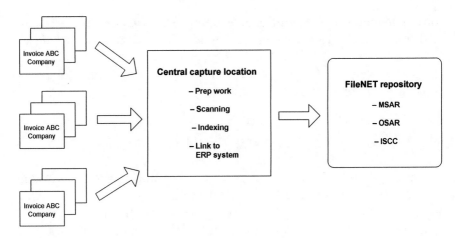

Figure 3.1
Centralized data capture

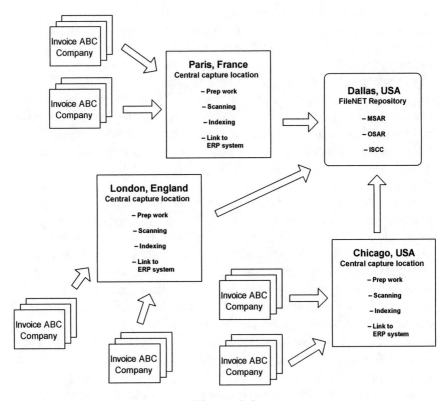

Figure 3.2
Decentralized data capture

products work well; however, developing a plan and getting accurate cost estimates can be a challenge because FileNet renames its products so many times. The goal of many of these products is the extension of Image Server services to remote locations, while staying in sync with the main Image Server through replication.

Disaster Recovery

When looking at imaging systems, many organizations quickly discount optical platters as a good media choice because of the increased reliability of cheap magnetic disk systems and the poorer performance of optical retrieval. FileNet built its imaging strategy on optical systems and continues to push these systems for the WORM capabilities that they provide. FileNet did not approach optical platters as just another storage medium; it focused on developing an imaging system that exploits optical media for its natural business fit, including regulatory compliance, archiving, and disaster recovery.

In the event of a disaster, a FileNet system can be completely restored from its duplicate optical media platters, known as *tranlogs*. These secondary optical platters are defined when setting up a document family and intended to be stored off-site. The tranlog platters contain not only the images but also a copy of the permanent database structure and the index (meta)data that belong to the individual document images. In fact, to assure there is *no* possibility of losing a backup image, the tranlog (backup) is created *before* creating the image for retrieval.

Despite FileNet's traditional reliance on the optical technology, the company has broadened its focus of storage to innovative magnetic storage solutions as well. Just remember to watch out for what appears to be a bias toward optical storage by the FileNet sales force.

When defining a list of potential disasters or series of disasters, either natural or human-made, the list becomes quite long. In fact, it is probably impossible to determine in advance what disasters will occur in the future. Business continuance, since September 11, has been the focus of many organizations. Disasters happen, the question is: Will an organization faced with a disaster survive?

Two basic strategies are involved in organizational planning for a disaster, recovery and business continuation. The first strategy (disaster recovery) focuses on plans to restart the business after a disas-

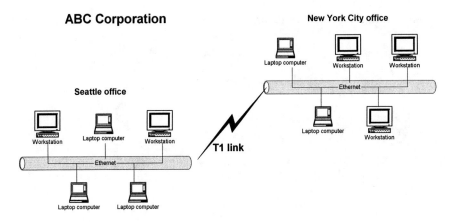

Figure 3.3
Single-link construction

ter; the other (business continuance) focuses on not allowing business to be stopped by a disaster. These philosophies are very different, even though often lumped together in the disaster planning category.

Good disaster planning requires asking the right questions:

- What if it all disappeared?
- How long can the organization survive without this resource?
- What is actually likely to occur?

In Figure 3.3, the two offices within the ABC Corporation are linked by a single T1 link. If the link goes down, regardless of any tape backup solutions, the two offices will not be able to communicate with data capture employees working on location. This is a major disaster. If the business process of the ABC Corporation requires these two offices to be in continual communication, they would experience a disaster with the loss of the T1 link.

To remedy this single point of failure, a second link could be set up with a completely different route to protect against a natural disaster breaking both links, as in Figure 3.4. However, a citywide power failure or a natural disaster in either city could still put the corporation's survival at risk.

Can the organization afford to be without the resource for only a few hours, up to one day, or for a week or more? Regardless of how

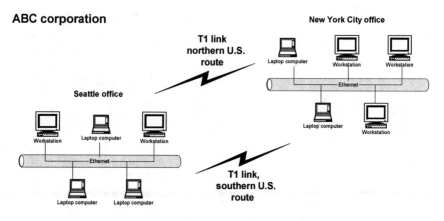

Figure 3.4
Dual-link construction

this question is answered, an organization builds a false security because it has identified the wrong resources to focus on. Many disaster plans focus on saving the data at all cost, because you can always bring in new equipment. The fact is, in more than 90% of all disasters, the equipment is undamaged. *Most actual outages are a failure of the utility infrastructure (power and telecom).* Even though the organization's data are secure and new equipment is available, the disaster does not end, because the disaster's victim is an external resource.

Most outages are tied to a failure of the utility infrastructure. However, an organization or individual should not draw the conclusion that, to avoid disaster, it should stick to paper processes and documents. Although electricity is not needed to read a paper document, the cost of using paper processes and the even greater threat of access losses can bring an organization to its knees without a disaster.

Another issue is that many organizations allow their tape systems to give them a false sense of security. A common misconception is that all the backup routines do read-back validity checks. This means that, if daily backups end without logging any errors, then you can be sure your data are protected. Sadly, this is often not the case. Many backups are created and maintained with the utmost optimism, but when it comes to disaster planning, optimism can be a dangerous thing.

Understand that there is no easy, fix-all solution. Disaster recovery and business continuance strategies can be extremely expensive, so individuals and teams have to balance the competing objectives of need and cost to determine a proper solution for their organization. Usually, the most critical systems demand high availability. In this case, it is almost always cheaper to plan for both high availability and disaster recovery simultaneously.

Lost Cost of Paper Retrieval

Some things in business are not challenged as often as they should be; one of these key areas is paper-based information systems. Information is vital to the formation of new knowledge, and knowledge is critical for the understanding of patterns. (For more information on pattern recognition and abstraction please refer to Chapter 5 of *Introduction to Knowledge Management—KM in Business* by Todd R. Groff and Thomas P. Jones [Butterworth–Heinemann, 2003]) Operating an organization using a paper-based system is similar to operating a mechanical engine without a lubricant, it creates friction that drains power and damages the overall system structure.

Paper-based processes drain the attention of employees, since they spend too much time and attention attempting to retrieve lost or misplaced documents. Although every nickel spent on an imaging system has to demonstrate ROI, the same rules do not apply to paper-based systems. This is not recommending the blind imaging of all available paper documents. However, it does speak well for the practice of treating proposed paper-based systems with the same level of rigor given to new content management system proposals.

Key factors in determining the ROI of imaging paper documents is the age of the document, the amount of times it is retrieved, and its retention life. Younger documents have a much greater chance of retrieval than older documents, and documents that have exceeded their retention life should be shredded, not imaged, for legal reasons. Another key point is the number of retrievals. The more times a document is retrieved from the system, the more valuable it is to image, due to the speed and efficiency of image retrieval over pulling a document from a file cabinet.

When weighing the usefulness of documents, involve the individuals that use the information everyday. Another important group is the data owners that set the retention policy for the documents in question. Sometimes these data owners come from a formal records retention group, other times they are a more tactical part of the business process. Seeking input from the legal department is also critical. In this day of rapidly increasing regulation of corporate financial policies, professional legal input is invaluable in determining what information simply must be maintained.

If the end of the retention time is a few years out, imaging the documents or information can help prevent the unauthorized access and proliferation of the documents. Paper tends to duplicate itself through the individuals' desire to maintain their own repository of files. This poses a risk to organizations by circumventing the official retention policy. Imaging systems can suffer the same issues with repository duplication, if printing is enabled through the client software and not discouraged actively. Typically, some users decide that they need to print and file every document with which they deal.

The risks and costs of this "prophylactic printing" seem minor to the user, who does not see the negative aggregate effects. Organizations tend to focus their security energy on limiting access to information instead of controlling the duplication of information outside of the defined system. This often means that ROI estimates based on floor space savings and reduced printing costs, mysteriously fail to occur.

CONTENT MANAGEMENT'S IMPACT ON ATTENTION

A discussion about the untracked costs in paper-based systems would not be complete without contrasting these losses to the gains of an imaging and document management system. Looking again to attention as the currency of the information age, it makes sense that the relationships that you build are affected by the drive to protect or the desire to earn attention.

Vendor relations are affected by how the vendor's attention is managed. From the beginning of a relationship with a vendor, processes for conflict resolution need to be well documented and communicated by both parties. When a conflict arises, sticking to the policies is critical to prevent the wasting of time, trust, and attention.

Before beginning an argument with a vendor, try to make sure that an airtight case is put together. Trust and attention are bound together: If you waste a vendor's time with an unspecific gripe, you waste the company's attention and reduce the amount of trust in the relationship. As trust is in a relationship is wasted, it has a negative impact on the passion for effective performance. If you have ever been unfortunate enough to work for a micromanager, you have witnessed this effect personally. As the micromanager constantly disregards employees' input, they begin to think, "Why should I care, I had no role in the process that led to this decision."

Content management systems can improve vendor relationships by providing an easily accessible repository for maintaining things like statement of work documents, vendor contact lists, contracts, and service-level agreements (SLA) (see Figure 3.5). Without a content management system, the information may be stranded in the desk drawers of project managers, technical workers, and contract negotiators. If improving a system costs the vendor loads of time just trying to find basic system details, it may simply not bother to invest its attention.

Another important aspect of attention management with vendors is seizing the opportunity to raise the level of understanding and generate a dialog within your own organization about attention management. The better a team understands and manages attention, the sooner that team will spot vendors that have no respect for the team's attention or that of its customers. Despite a vendor's claims or testimonials, if it does not value your attention, doing business with it represents a significant risk to your project's ROI.

Five ways to spot vendors that do not value attention:

1. Companies that constantly send spam or junk mail to potential customers.
2. Companies that miss appointments or insist in always meeting in person.
3. Organizations that use the Internet only to provide a completely uninteractive billboard. They typically make available only *marketing* information anyway.

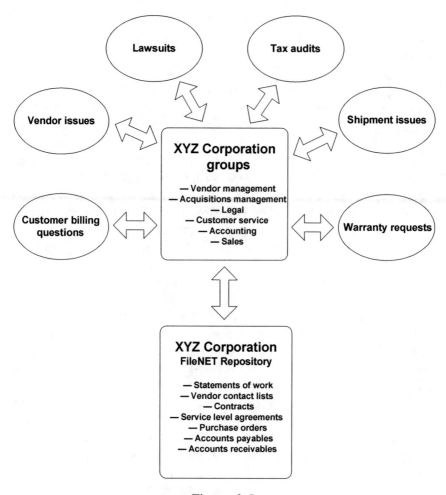

Figure 3.5
Content management and attention

4. Organizations that insist on generating week's worth of contract negotiations for selling their base products.
5. Organizations or companies that want to deal with you strictly via voice, with no long-term record.

There are some exceptions to this hard-line approach to potential "attention depleters." For example, is the organization new or is the attention-wasting happening only with the sales force? Also, unfortunately, in the business world, you often have little choice but to do your best to work with attention wasters, despite their obsolete procedures.

INTELLECTUAL ASSETS

Another reason for companies to use content management is the opportunity to manage their intellectual assets. Intellectual assets include information like trademarks, copyright, patents, industrial designs, trade secrets, confidential information, detailed analysis documents, and other knowledge resources that add value not only to processes but also to the overall organization. The vital corporate information on which a corporation's survival depends must be protected against unauthorized destruction, copying, and alteration, and in some cases, disclosure.

Companies pursue patents for reasons that often extend beyond directly profiting from a patented innovation through either its commercialization or licensing. Popular motives for patenting intellectual assets include preventing rivals from patenting related inventions, using patents to influence merger negotiations, and the prevention of lawsuits. Managing an enterprise's intellectual assets is more than just acquiring the formal intellectual property (IP) rights from the local governing authority. Patent or trademark rights are worthless to the company if they are not exploited to meet business objectives.

Intellectual capital may be exploited in a variety of ways, including commercializing patent protected products and services, developing new and creative licensing or franchising partnerships, selling IP assets to other companies, gaining access to other companies' technology through cross-licensing, and leveraging IP assets to borrow money. Determining how organizations might best exploit their IP assets will have to be done case by case.

Throughout history, organizations have been taken over for their assets. Businesses often buy out their competitors to gain process knowledge, experienced craft workers, or physical assets such as land, buildings, or equipment. A clear policy on enforcing intellectual property rules is crucial, due to the losses incurred by counterfeited goods and the potential high costs of IP litigation. A strong content management system is essential for locating, storing, and automating the sharing of intellectual assets. Do not doubt that poor intellectual asset management could pose a huge risk to a company.

RECORDS RETENTION

Records retention is often overlooked when building a content management plan. Most companies have records retention strategies, but sometimes they can be disconnected from the imaging strategy. An imaging plan can have a serious impact on records retention if not handled properly.

Defining Document Life Cycles

A records retention policy should exist whether an organization maintains imaging or paper systems. Documents have a life cycle and, in most cases, should be destroyed at the end of that life cycle. Maintaining outdated archives can negatively affect an organization in many ways; formalizing a records retention policy is always a better solution.

Most records retentions systems assign a unique ID to every box of paper documents that enters its realm of responsibility. This ID is a good reference point for tying together the paper and the electronic image. Tying together the image and the paper, in an organization that maintains both, is critical to ensure that one or the other does not exist beyond the document's life cycle. Figure 3.6 is a flowchart on how a records retention system and a content management system could work together. You can see that, regardless of where the box of documents enters the process, it has the option of being imaged. The paper then resides in the Record Retention department's storage area until it is destroyed.

Often, for legal reasons, the paper must be maintained, but paper does not flow well through business processes. The best answer is to image the paper, keep the paper in a low-cost retention center, and use the images in the workflow. If the images are no longer needed at the end of their life cycle, query on the box number and delete all those files in one batch.

This brings up an important issue. How do you destroy images stored in WORM optical format? The objective of WORM technol-

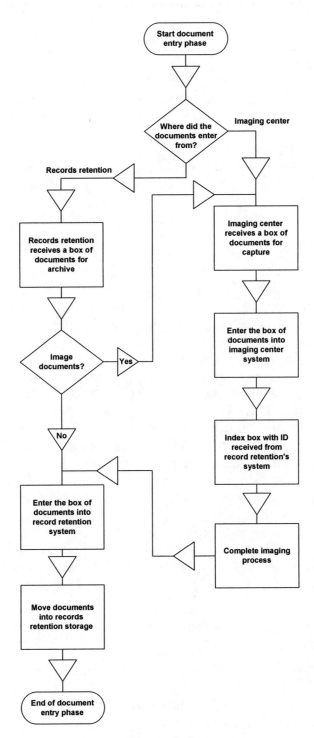

Figure 3.6
Records retention flowchart

ogy is to assure that permanent storage will not allow changes to fixed content. However, companies face significant litigation risks for not purging old, obsolete information and documents.

One option is the destruction of the WORM platter itself; however, this requires careful monitoring of every document written on the platter to ensure that all the documents have reached the end of the life cycle. This option also requires more upfront planning and administration. A lack of planning in the implementation phase could lead to documents not being destroyed on time or drastically increasing media costs.

When considering the option of destroying WORM media, keep in mind that "document families" within FileNet define where and how the data are written. This becomes vital when destroying records. At some point, most WORM optical platters have to be destroyed to assure that the information on them cannot be recovered. If only a portion of the documents on the platter have reached the end of their life cycles, then destroying the platter probably is no option. Figure 3.7 shows the relationship.

In the figure, one document family contains three document classes. If the three document classes represent invoices, e-mail, and project documents, you would assume that they need to be retained for different lengths of time. Perhaps, e-mail would have a very short retention period and project documents a very long retention period. Unfortunately, when the retention period ends for the e-mail, they might have to be maintained long after their set deletion date, because all the classes in a document family reside on the same optical platter. You cannot destroy the optical media on which the e-mails is stored on without also destroying project documents and invoices, if all are in the same document family.

A better plan is to use a magnetic disk rather than an optical platter for the tranlogs. FileNet produces a magnetic storage and retrieval

Document Classes	Document Classes	Document Classes
Document Families		
Defines storage (If optical platters, it will combine document classes within the same family on the same platters)		

Figure 3.7
Document families and classes

option as well as other partner options. EMC's Centera product works with FileNet Image Manager (formerly Image Services) 4.01 to provide what EMC calls *content-addressed storage*. This allows Centera to manage the retention of FileNet documents at the record level rather than at the level of each individual unit of media, which makes it an ideal option for avoiding the limitations of optical storage.

FileNet's MSAR solution was engineered to work as closely to their OSAR solution as possible and to meet WORM standards. The strengths of the MSAR solution over the OSAR include reduced maintenance and improved access speed. The downside is that FileNet usually sells you a small optical system for backups.

Experience has shown that removal of the robotics (optical units) from an imaging system can reduce downtime by as much as 15%. Maintenance to disk systems is often as easy as adding or replacing drives that are "hot swappable." This means that many repairs can be made with no inconvenience or downtime for the end users. The single-arm architecture of most optical units makes repairs without downtime nearly impossible.

The EMC Centera product uses multiple servers in a grid computing configuration to assure that the data are not only readily available but can be configured for disaster recovery. Data integrity is checked after each retrieval, and the system also checks integrity constantly during off-peak hours. This makes the system ideal for high-availability needs in organizations that cannot tolerate significant downtime.

In addition to the benefits that are associated with magnetic disk systems, the issue of document life cycles is an important topic for discussion. Remember, optical platters, depending on their configuration, may contain more than one document class' data. This, again, is not a technical issue as much as it is a planning issue.

FileNet document classes are typically used to define security boundaries surrounding a department, subdivision, or sector. Project managers request the setup of a new document class surrounding a new area of responsibility. Often, the document family is overlooked. A good FileNet administrator, when administrating a FileNet system containing optical storage units, will raise the archival issues surrounding having multiple document classes tied to a single document family.

Figure 3.8 shows different ways to segregate document classes with document families within FileNet. As the diagram shows, the break

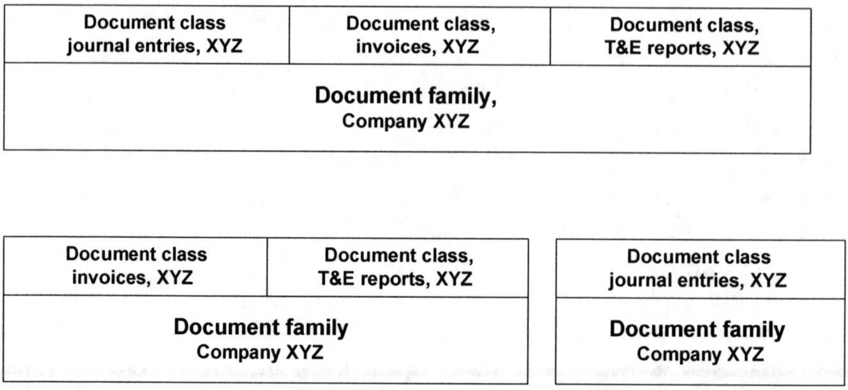

Document class journal entries, XYZ	Document class, invoices, XYZ	Document class, T&E reports, XYZ
Document family, Company XYZ		

Document class invoices, XYZ	Document class, T&E reports, XYZ		Document class journal entries, XYZ
Document family Company XYZ			**Document family** Company XYZ

Figure 3.8

Document families and classes, segregation by family

in document families is more often a business call than a technical issue. An outsourcing provider may choose to set up document families based on the customer's company. That would allow the outsourcing provider to easily export all of a customer's data by simply giving the customer their optical disks.

When reviewing the life cycle of documents to be captured through a process being defined or automated, it is important to include records retention. The reason for this is existing knowledge. Most Records Retention departments have already spent the necessary time and energy to classify existing organizational document life cycles. Records Retention departments often have existing relationships with the corporate legal department to assure strong regulatory compliance and avoid policies that may lead to litigation. As an imaging or document management project comes online, it should always have defined the key archival and destruction processes. Do not reinvent the wheel—collaborate.

Records Retention departments need to track containers entrusted with key information, including information on the unique identification number, owner of container's contents, when the container was archived, length of archive, who to notify with issues, who to notify when container has reached the end of its archival time, who has authorization to access the container, and whether or not there are image copies of the contents of the container. If a Records

Retention department lacks a database system to track this information, FileNet's imaging or content management products can fill this need.

The Process of Destruction

At the end of its life cycle, the document and all its copies should be destroyed. This may sound like a relatively straightforward process; however, whenever an organization attempts to do anything with unstructured data, it is quickly apparent that the procedures for manipulating structured data fall apart. Adding to this complexity are the optical issues touched upon previously.

Most organizations, when approaching the issues surrounding records retention and unstructured data, quickly realize the need to lay out their objectives in writing. Organizing the objectives helps speed along dialog and reduces the chance of wasting the attention of the individuals involved. Normally, what comes from these dialogs is a realization of the competing objectives within the organization surrounding unstructured data. The following is an example of some competing issues:

- Need to improve efficiency by imaging departmental paper.
- Documents must be destroyed within one year of their creation.
- Need to keep the original paper document for audit purposes.
- Need to store all images using WORM technology.
- Need to limit access to these documents.
- Need to access these documents globally.

This short list is common among imaging and document management projects and similar regardless of the organizational function. Figure 3.9 presents a sample workflow for destroying paper and electronic documents.

The figure begins with the decision to verify with the customer that all documents reaching the end of their archive life actually should be destroyed. The sample workflow assumes that a system is used to track archived documents. Typically, when the end of the archive is flagged, documents are not automatically destroyed without final

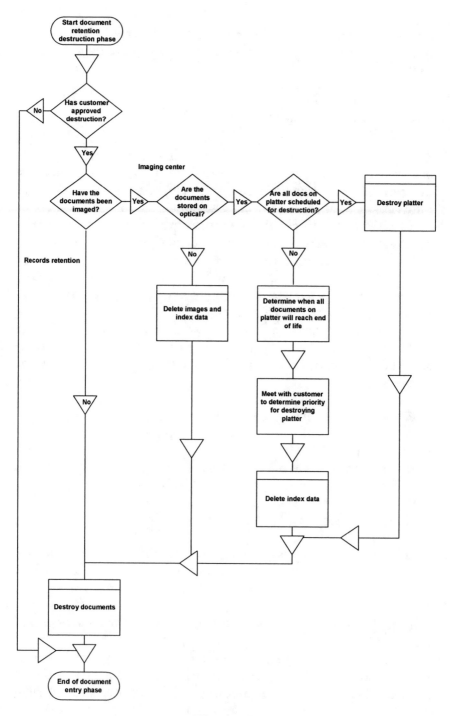

Figure 3.9
Records destruction flowchart

customer approval. This is important because document life cycles sometimes change. New regulations or ongoing court proceedings may require keeping large amounts of documents beyond their initially defined retention period.

Next, a decision must be made and documented to determine if imaging was used on these documents. The imaging decision should be documented in the records retention system, as a field tied to the document container record to make sure that the information is readily available. If the documents have not been imaged, then only the paper records need to be destroyed.

If the documents were imaged, the process gets more complicated. Information must be included that describes how the images were stored (on optical or magnetic media). If the images are stored on optical platters, it is important to remember that records cannot be individually erased from an optical WORM platter. So, before destroying the optical platter, all the documents must be ready for deletion, including any corresponding tranlog platters. While waiting for other documents to reach the end of their life cycles, the index record within FileNet can be altered to prevent simple access to the document.

If the images are not stored on optical media, then the images, along with the index record, can be destroyed with much less difficulty. The biggest concern is backup tapes. An organization's retention plan benefits from the input of all available stakeholders and the considerations of imaging and paper documents in the retention plan. Retention audits should also be conducted to test the procedures in action.

SUCCESS STORY

An international building and construction materials supplier heavily involved supporting Australia's growth must streamline its accounts payable (A/P) and accounts receivable (A/R) processes. The company generates 1000 A/P documents, 4000 A/R invoices, and 500 customer remittances each day.

To maintain its growth, the company needs to streamline its paper-based processes. The materials supplier hires FileNet to develop a solution, and together they implement an ECM solution utilizing image services and capture professional. The solution utilizes optical disks and server cache for storage and a thin client for search, retrieval, faxing, and e-mail.

This solution enables the organization to accomplish the following:

- Recognize a reoccurring savings of $1 million per year by reducing the A/R processing time.
- Improve search and retrieval from invoice archives.
- Improve customer satisfaction and reduce customer frustration.
- Improve monthly cash flow.

Chapter 4

FILENET
IMPLEMENTATION

The trouble with learning from experience is that the test comes
first and the lesson comes afterwards!

—Anonymous

KEY OBJECTIVES

■ Learn to develop well-documented return-on-investment goals
and strategies long before a technology is settled on.
■ Learn what levels of resources are required to support administration, processing, storage, and collaboration within a
FileNet system.
■ Understand why teams become increasingly ineffective in a
corporate "star culture," which overemphasizes the input of
articulate specialists.
■ Consider the options for data replication within a FileNet
implementation and choose the one that best meets the project
requirements.
■ Learn the differences between precommittal, postcommittal,
and simultaneous indexing.
■ Know the pros and cons of the various storage media offered
for FileNet systems.

- Understand what project planning questions you must answer before choosing a media storage format.
- Learn what "gotchas" to watch for when setting up FileNet hardware.
- Increase your knowledge of the basic architecture of any FileNet system.
- Know the critical first steps involved in any FileNet implementation.

CONTENT MANAGEMENT VERSUS PROCESS VOODOO

Too often, companies look to content management or knowledge management as a solution for all for their organizational problems. *Voodoo* usually refers to the delusive assumption that using a charm, fetish, or spell can achieve the normally unachievable. Within large organizations it is not unusual to see similar phony solutions offered to solve fundamental process problems. They are often recognizable by the speed at which they arrive. It is charmingly tempting to apply the "solution of the week" quickly, while shutting down any valuable stakeholder discussions of the issues involved. Although this helps avoid some painfully tense meetings, it typically leads to only symptomatic solutions, best. This "process voodoo" may have worked in the late 1990s to increase an organization's stock price, but today it is just a lot of smoke and mirrors.

Today's organizations need to focus on what has always made companies great, not merely what increased their stock during the boom. People are the key asset of any organization, not just the top 12 employees but all of the organization's employees down to the lowest level. Valuing people as assets has been the proven ingredient for success in most organizational success stories.

Content management and knowledge management improve an organization's ability to capture and distribute individual ideas and feedback. This leads to more dialog, better strategies, and a more satisfied workforce. Building a repository can also demonstrate an individual's knowledge of subjects and jobs not currently in his or her job description. A worker's title rarely expresses the diversity of skills and experience available.

Implementing systems to store this information and executing events to spur and capture dialog and documents is not enough.

Attention must be valued and rewarded. Individuals must be valued by their organization and see the organization valuing their input for the dialog to be both valuable and sustainable. Knowledge management should not be merely a buzzword to move the stock price forward; that is not a sustainable business plan.

A very good place to start building small content or knowledge repositories is when executing a project. A knowledge base is not the actual storage of knowledge but the storage of information that demonstrates an individual or group's knowledge about the project or process around which the knowledge base was designed. FileNet or any other configurable content manager can be used for these knowledge bases, but the key is to plan carefully and use what is readily available. Do not focus your initial energies on shopping for technologies but on capturing the information that offers the greatest potential to improve performance.

The knowledge base is also an excellent tool to be passed from a project team to an administrative team. Even the simple act of showing team members that there is a common, shared document repository can build trust. In many companies, project plans are created in secrecy to serve goals that the project manager does not even want to admit to the team members. It should come with little surprise that the teams usually end up paralyzed by constant political battles.

Most processes continue to evolve with time, but if the process knowledge that leads to evolution is tied to one team, like the administrative team, then the group responsible for project delivery is excluded and continues using outdated facts, knowledge, and processes. Figure 4.1 shows how knowledge must be passed along to different groups as a business process moves through its lifecycle. The way an organization handles projects, knowledge, and learning is a key indicator of that organization's sustainability. Dialog around process change and the documenting of processes in a commonly used knowledge base helps create the learning basis for innovation within an organization.

Information Repositories

Building information repositories is a long-term commitment of significant budget dollars that should be well thought out before being undertaken. Well-documented ROI goals and strategies should be

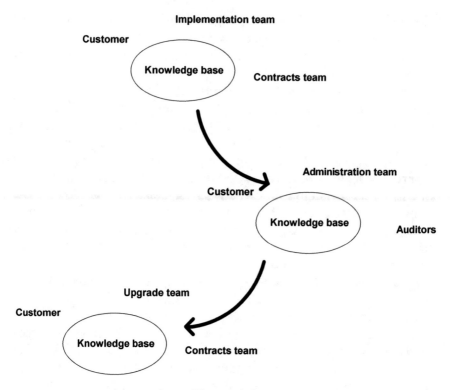

Figure 4.1
Reusable knowledge

developed and discussed long before a technology is settled on. If the repository is being developed for knowledge management, even more thought and dialog should be expended, due to the evolutionary level that knowledge management is at currently. The world has entered an information age; however, the tools currently available to manage information and create knowledge exchange are very primitive. Sadly, the most commonly used document management system is still the paper clip.

FileNet's product lines can assist an organization in the following areas of enterprise content management: process management, imaging management, workflow tools, Web content and document management, and knowledge management. Keep in mind that the necessary resources vary by implementation, need, and resource type. Table 4.1 outlines the resource requirements by component.

Table 4.1
Enterprise Content Management Resource Requirements

	Administration	Processors	Storage	Collaboration
Imaging management	Low	Low	High	Low
Web content and document management	Medium	Low	Low	High
Workflow tools	Low	High	Low	High
Process management		Low	Low	High
Knowledge management	Medium	High	Low	High

Some of the most successful knowledge management initiatives have been focused on people development instead of system development. Knowledge resides in people not systems, but people, like systems, must be developed to achieve their full potential. Through the content management, search, collaboration, and learning tools FileNet provides, new internal channels are created to spur knowledge exchange and dialog. This leads workers to the understanding that their documents are valued and the time they invest in creating them is not wasted.

Many companies use simple directory tools to manage contact information on their employees, while offering the ability to search the directory for specific expertise. Locating their own experts when they need them is a common challenge in large organizations. This is why millions are spent every year on people development initiatives like communities of practice, training classes, and mentoring programs.

People development initiatives can also have drawbacks, such as creating a "star culture." Many large organizations have historically relied on star talent to succeed. The star culture is typically made up of educated, articulate specialists, who are encouraged to pursue business initiatives unconstrained by the traditional checks and balances of organizational business units. The "stars" often can get quick results through the circumventing of existing bureaucracies; however, bureaucracies exist for a reason: They represent checks and balances for maintaining order and audits within an organization. Circumventing bureaucracies create many issues that require time-consuming cleanup and are not a sustainable practice, but the key issue with the star culture is the possible erosion of key organizational processes that could put that organization in violation of regulatory statutes such as the Sarbanes-Oxley Act.

FileNet Replication Options

Organizations today face the issues of an increasingly global economy and workforce. The issues surrounding a global economy and workforce can paralyze an organization's planning committees. This section addresses using FileNet's imaging products in a globally distributed environment. Two important terms to understand are *precommittal indexing* and *postcommittal indexing*. Both deal with the point at which the indexing is completed on an image (object). If the indexing is completed prior to the image (object) being committed to media (while still being stored in Batch Entry Services cache), then it is considered precommittal indexing. If the indexing is completed after the image (object) has been committed (moved from Batch Entry Services cache to the Page cache and burned to the OSAR or written to the MSAR) then it is considered postcommittal indexing.

Precommittal indexing:

■ Is indexed using FileNet's Capture product.
■ Works in the Batch Entry Services (BES) cache.
■ Requires the Batch Entry Services cache to be accessible by both scanner and indexer.

Postcommittal indexing:

■ Is indexed as a reindex, using FileNet's Panagon client application.
■ Works in the Page cache.
■ Requires the Batch Entry Services cache to be accessible by scanner and Page cache to be accessible by indexer.

Definitions

BES cache. This cache is used during the capture phase of imaging by the scanners and indexers (precommittal indexing). Once a batch is completed, it is "committed" to the OSAR. This means it is written to optical storage media and copied to Page cache.

Page cache. This cache facilitates quick retrieval by maintaining recently created or accessed items to prevent the need to repeatedly retrieve the same image from optical storage. Items are kept according to FIFO (first in/first out) rules. Reindexing happens in Page cache, but the new index information is maintained only in the Oracle database. Only the original index properties are burned to the OSAR's optical platters.

Figure 4.2 shows the replication points in a FileNet system using postcommittal indexing.

This figure demonstrates a postcommittal indexing scenario in an offshore environment. The process is numbered and described by step:

1. Documents are normally prepared for scanning and the preparation stage typically includes staple removal, paper preparation, and some sorting into batches. Scanning is completed using FileNet's Capture application, and the batches are committed to the FileNet Root Server (Image Manager, formerly

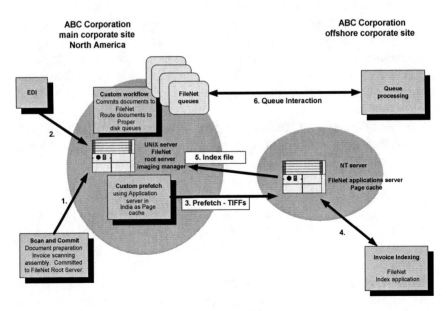

Figure 4.2
Postcommittal indexing

Image Services). Once committed, a copy of the document is written to the Page cache and a copy is written to primary storage. This may be either an OSAR or MSAR unit.

2. Electronic Data Interchange (EDI) documents are received through FileNet's fax services and loaded into a predefined template. They can have predefined indexing or be indexed later with the other postcommittal indexing jobs.

3. Documents are prefetched (copied) to the application server at the offshore location and stored in a secondary Page cache. The application server has several FileNet names, including Application Server, Remote Entry Server, Batch Entry Services, and Distributed Image Services. Regardless of the name, it is a scaled-down version of the Image Manager (formerly Image Services). The application server does not contain a copy of the FileNet Root Server's security database and cannot authenticate users.

4. In this step, the documents are indexed at an offshore location. The actual process, called *reindexing*, uses the standard FileNet client to perform this function. Note that only the Oracle database is changed or added to during this process. The original index, stored within the primary storage media (OSAR or MSAR), remains the same. For this reason, tape backups of the Oracle databases should be taken a minimum of every day.

5. Once the reindex has been completed, the remote Page cache automatically updates the Oracle database stored on the FileNet Root Server (Image Manager server formerly Image Services server).

6. After indexing is completed, workflow can be initiated to populate FileNet's distributor queues and interconnect with any exiting ERP (enterprise resource planning) system.

Figure 4.3 looks into precommittal indexing.

This figure demonstrates a precommittal indexing scenario in an offshore environment. The process is numbered and described by step:

1. Documents are normally prepared for scanning, and the preparation stage typically includes staple removal, paper preparation, and the like. Scanning is completed using FileNet's

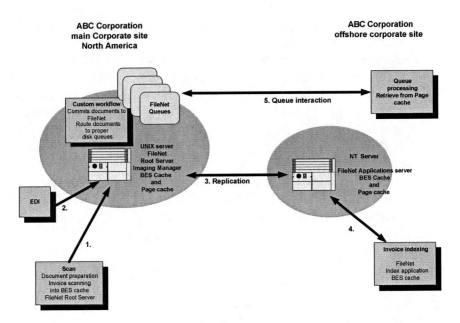

Figure 4.3
Precommittal indexing

Capture application, and the batch remains in the FileNet Root Server's BES cache awaiting indexing.

2. EDI documents are received through FileNet's fax services and loaded into a predefined template. They can have predefined indexing and be automatically committed or manually indexed in a precommittal indexing scenario.

3. Documents are replicated using FileNet's replication to the application server at the offshore location and stored in an external BES cache. The application server has several FileNet names, including Application Server, Remote Entry Server, Batch Entry Services, and Distributed Image Services. Regardless of the name, it is a scaled-down version of the Image Manager (formerly Image Services). The application server contains no copy of the FileNet Root Server's security database and cannot authenticate users.

4. This section represents the indexing of the documents at a remote offshore location. The indexing process uses FileNet's

Capture client to perform this function. During the indexing stage, the BES cache is updated on the remote application server and later replicated back to the FileNet Root Server's BES cache. When the indexing process is complete, the indexer "commits the document." The committal process moves the image and index out of the BES cache to the Page cache and writes (commits) the document and index to primary and secondary storage (OSAR for optical, MSAR or Centera solution for magnetic).

5. After indexing and commitment is completed, the workflow can be initiated to populate FileNet's distributor queues and interconnect with any existing ERP system.

Media Options

In the previous sections, discussion touched on media options without supplying a complete picture. There are currently several options for storage media and more to be released before this book sees print. For this reason, the options are not discussed in depth. However, Figure 4.4 should be helpful in understanding the categories of options an organization has to choose from.

FileNet's Image Manager product requires the separate purchase of media drivers based on the organizations retention strategy. If an organization's direction is optical storage, then an OSAR media driver would be purchased, based on the optical media options chosen. The media options are based on third-party offerings and not controlled by FileNet. FileNet participates in the high-end optical market, but its imaging media options are not required for a successful implementation. These options work equally well with Hewlett Packard products.

The current media driver options are OSAR, MSAR, and a Professional Services ISCC (Image Services Connector for Centera) media driver for EMC's Centera. This last driver is currently being packaged for release in FileNet's Image Manager 4.1 version.

Moving from left to right, the Imaging Management application in the figure is provided by FileNet. FileNet provides the media drivers today, but this could change in the not-so-distant future. Lastly, the media options are mainly provided by third-party vendors, however, FileNet does offer OSARs.

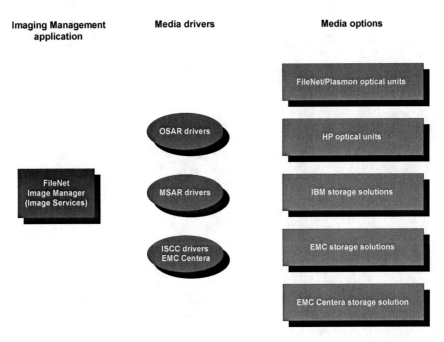

Figure 4.4
Media options

Table 4.2 is a high-level look at the media choice options offered for FileNet's Image Manager product line. Keep in mind that this is only a glimpse of the solutions and configurations possible, given the large number of FileNet partners that have individually customized FileNet systems.

Inquiry and Investigation

Before choosing an imaging media, it is advisable to ask FileNet to provide contacts for customers in related fields using FileNet with various media types. Site visits are recommended but a teleconference could at least cover the big questions. Relevant questions include:

■ What is the configuration of your organization's FileNet system?
■ What product and version of FileNet's product lines are being used?

Table 4.2

MSAR, EMC Centera, and OSAR Comparison

MSAR	ISCC (EMC Centera)	OSAR
PROs	PROs	PROs
Storage media can be shared with other applications	Storage media can be shared with other applications	Proven history of regulatory compliance
Much quicker retrieval than optical platform	Self-managing and easier to maintain, for a lower cost of ownership	Tranlog capabilities for burning and storing off-site copies is built-in
Scalable, with a wider selection of equipment than optical platform	WORM-like retention for regulatory compliance (can be deleted only after specified retention period)	Metadata capture at committal stored on the platter
Seamless integration into Image Manager	Much quicker retrieval than optical platform	Removable media
Can generate tranlogs remotely for disaster planning and recovery	Scalable, with a wider selection of equipment than optical platform	Seamless integration into Image Manager
WORM compliant if combined with an OSAR solution	Requires no media migration when expanding storage	
	Has built-in data redundancy	
CONs	CONs	CONs
Not WORM compliant by itself	Not addressed as a file system, requires interface via EMC application program interfaces	High cost of initial purchase, media, and maintenance
May still require extra disk equipment for cross-committal, tape, or optical disk for disaster recovery	May still require extra Centera equipment, tape, or optical disk for disaster recovery	Slower retrieval than magnetic platform
		Robotic arm (only one, no backup) will fail
		Media migrations required every time an upgrade changes the hardware

- Can a data capture process overview be provided?
- What media and media drivers are being used with the FileNet system?
- Is there a disaster backup plan or a business continuation plan?
- How does the media fit the disaster backup or business continuation plan?
- Did the organization research the legal ramifications of using this specific media from the local, state, and federal levels?
- Is this system accessed from multiple states or countries? If so, did this affect or cause any legal issues?
- Has the organization been through any hardware upgrades since the initiation of the FileNet system?
- Did the media type chosen for the FileNet system require Professional Services migration?
- What is the expected retrieval time for a three-to-five page image within the organization? Is this a problem within the organization?
- What would you change about the FileNet implementation?

These sample questions could be e-mailed ahead of time to the existing FileNet customer. Although this may seem like a lot of work for the existing user, it provides the opportunity to learn from an organization planning a FileNet installation. The responding company can learn what new products FileNet is promoting, along with the differences in processes.

SPECIALTY EQUIPMENT CONSIDERATIONS

When planning an imaging implementation or any implementation that requires an optical storage unit, some items should be given extra attention. Implementations of optical units are not as simple and straightforward as the setup of a server or network device. A project manager should order the OSAR two or three months ahead of the rest of the project equipment because of the complexity of the unit and its installation.

The large optical storage and retrieval unit market is controlled mainly by Plasmon, which builds units sold by FileNet. The current models range in capacity from around 3 terabytes to 3.6 terabytes. The high-end cost for an OSAR unit is around $300,000 (which does not include the media cost). Purchasing 12″ storage media for an optical unit has an approximate cost of $65,000, which works out to about $0.10 per megabyte. Optical media costs twice that of magnetic media, so any implementation based on optical storage needs to be handled properly to keep the implementation costs under control.

Service contracts on a typical FileNet/Plasmon OSAR are approximately $50,000 per year on a high-end six-drive unit.

The typical steps for implementing an OSAR unit include:

- Ordering the OSAR several months in advance of the other equipment.
- Completing a service agreement with the maintenance service provider (typically the same group contracted to set up and configure the OSAR on delivery).
- Making any special arrangements for shipping and receiving this very large and heavy unit.
- Assembling the OSAR unit (which comes in pieces, to allow it to fit into most data centers, and must be assembled).
- Leveling the OSAR (normally, after assembly, the OSAR is leveled three or four times).
- Final testing and adjustments of sensors, cables, and drives.
- Loading production optical storage platters.

The main components of an optical storage and retrieval unit are:

106–122 30-GB optical platters storing data.
1 robotic arm to move platters from slots to drives.
1–6 optical drives for reading and writing data.

At a very high level the OSAR unit appears to be fairly simple. What the list does not include is the bushings, cables, rods, sensors, and other parts that can break or vibrate loose on an OSAR unit. A highly trained engineer must repair these. Optical units require shutdowns every six months for lubrication and preventive maintenance. Depending on the number of arm movements required in a day, preventive maintenance might be required more often. Luckily, a system with a sufficiently large Page cache can allow shutdown of the OSAR, with no interruption in service to the end users.

One way to extend the life of an OSAR unit is to build the FileNet Image Manager server with a lot of available Page cache. Page cache is where recently accessed or captured data are stored until the Page cache becomes full and forces it out. The Page cache uses the FIFO (first in/first out) method for managing its contents.

When a document is scanned, it is stored in the Batch Entry Services cache until it is indexed and committed. When a document is committed, it is copied to Page cache and written to the primary storage, which could be magnetic or optical. When sufficient read or write requests come through Page cache, the scanned document are pushed out of the Page cache by more recent read and write requests. When a request comes to the FileNet Image Manager server for the document, it is read into Page cache and sent to the requesting party or application. Documents always pass through Page cache as they are written to or read from the primary storage.

When using an OSAR unit for primary storage on an accounts payable imaging system, we recommend that the Page cache be large enough to hold at least six to nine months worth of images. This allows the invoice approvers to pull their images directly from the page cache—for speed. This also greatly reduces the wear and tear on the optical unit. In calculating six to nine months worth of Page cache, multiply the total number of invoices received in a month times the average number of pages per invoice times 50 KB.

This gives you an estimate of the total storage requirements in KB per month. Then, simple multiply the total KB per month by the total number of months that you want to be held in Page cache. This will give you the total amount of Page cache space that must be allocated.

If the project implementation plan includes multiple application servers, each with its own Page cache, it would make sense to use a custom prefetch utility to prefetch only the documents that each remote application server needs (see Figure 4.5). This avoids wasting Page cache on the individual application servers while providing the best retrieval times at the remote sites.

PROJECT PLANNING

Estimating Project Timelines

When estimating a project's costs and building a timeline for a FileNet product implementation, it is very important to allow time for FileNet contract negotiations and scheduling a FileNet resource

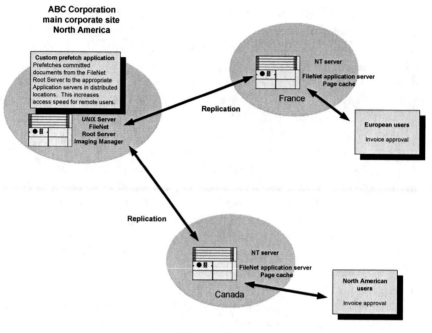

Figure 4.5
Prefetching to remote application servers

to complete the system installation (typically a four-week lead time).

Keep in mind that most FileNet products are just toolsets, not complete off-the-shelf solutions. Before building a document or imaging solution, first have a documented, proven, manual process that can be improved on and replaced by automated workflow tools. This gives you the metrics to track project ROI and provide a greater opportunity for success.

Project Plans

A project plan defines the scope of a work, with specific beginning and ending points. However, the process the project puts in place most likely continues long after the project has ended. Because of the differences between projects and processes, projects often creep in scope and processes often fail to continue to evolve.

In preparing for any implementation, some important issues must be addressed at the beginning of the project. Feel free to use the project-planning example that follows, as a starting point for your next project plan.

Phase 1. Project Preparation

During this step, the reason for the project as well as the initial funding and sponsorship are defined. Next, a project charter is created that includes the definition of the project team, project roles, organization, and a high level project plan.

The major steps of Phase 1 are:

- Defining the project goals and objectives.
- Establishing project sponsorship and initial assessment funding.
- Clarifying the scope of the project.
- Defining the overall project schedule and implementation sequence.
- Establishing the project organization, member roles, and subcommittees.
- Proposal of an implementation strategy.
- Initial cost assessments are created for approval.

Addressing these issues early in the project planning helps ensure the project proceeds efficiently and a solid foundation for a successful implementation is established.

Phase 2. Project Design

During this phase, a team is organized to develop a detailed plan from the initial assessment. A key task at this stage is to capture the assumptions of the team members as they are discovered and created. Assumptions should be explicitly listed in the documentation, and this documentation should be distributed widely. As each assumption is found to be either true or false, the project documentation should be updated accordingly. We call this *assumption management*.

The major steps of Phase 2 are:

- Assigning resources.
- Kicking off the project helps create awareness of the project within the organization. High-level project goals and visions for

the future are shared with key people from various parts of the organization.
- Defining project procedures.
- Documenting the project management and implementation standards, and defining the system landscape.
- Laying out the project-training plan, including a strategy for end-user training, and beginning the development of documentation.
- Defining the implementation steps.
- Developing plans for hardware procurement to meet the technical requirements of the system.
- Developing a business impact map, describing how the current business processes will be affected; this is done by the organizational change management group. Preparing organizational risk assessment documents to identify the risks that must be addressed to assure successful implementation.
- Building a training and development environment, often referred to as the sandbox, which the functional team can use for testing. This is done by infrastructure team members.
- Documenting and developing the master template for installation packaging using client settings and packaging.
- Setting up indexing workshops to determine which items of data must be tracked in the new system. Specify what is important today and determine if there is any need for additional fields or key fields.

Phase 3. Project Building

During this phase, the project plans are put into action. Systems are built, code is written, training materials are deployed, and communications are made in the project building phase.

A key requirement of this phase is the continuation of assumption management. During this phase, assumptions should be tested and proven while continuing to capture new assumptions as they are made and adding them to the assumption management process.

The major steps of Phase 3 are:

- Initial planning for production support (competency center/ help desk).

- Conducting team training and continuing development of end-user training documentation and training material.
- Performing baseline configuration, testing, and confirmation tasks.
- Creating a system management plan, including testing procedures, service-level commitments, setup of quality assurance and production systems, and assignment of system administration functions.
- Developing conversion programs to bring forward data from the legacy systems.
- Developing interface programs to connect to any external systems defined in the scope document.
- Creating metrics tracking reports.
- Establishing archiving schedules and procedures.

Phase 4. Testing, Training, and Implementation

The purpose of this phase is to complete the final implementation steps, including testing, end-user training, system management, and cutover activities prior to execution. The activity in this phase is the actual implementation. This phase also resolves all crucial open issues. On successful completion of this phase, the system is considered to be in production.

The major steps of Phase 4 are:

- Training and communication to help desk personnel assigned to support the new system.
- Performing system tests, including tests of system failure, system backup, system restoration, disaster recovery, production system printing, system volume, and system stress.
- Final checking, like a dress rehearsal for your processes.
- Conducting project planning activities, including refinement of the cutover plan, conversion checklist, refinement of the production support plan, final preparations on the help desk for full activation, and finally the cutover to production.

After the final check is passed, the system is considered to be in production mode.

Overall Project Estimates and Total Cost of Ownership (TCO)

When considering a FileNet implementation, it is important to remember that the workflow piece of FileNet's product line is just a tool. It will not fix broken processes, and it will not create new processes on its own. People must design the new processes and diagnose the broken ones.

FileNet is a good tool to use for the automation of working processes, but like many tools, it has limitations. One limitation is the lack of published material on the FileNet toolset. More than likely, if an organization is using FileNet's workflow for the first time, it would be wise to consider bringing in expert help for the initial design and setup. This appears costly the first time, but building knowledge and understanding of the workflow product in the organization will take time. Time, typically, is something projects lack most.

Projecting Support Cost Needs

One feature of FileNet that often seems overlooked is the relative low cost of administrative support. For instance, a large oil company with a worldwide presence manages a complex FileNet solution that is composed of three production UNIX servers. The system maintains more than $2\frac{1}{2}$ terabytes of data, using 12 NT servers to manage distributed capture, printing, faxing, and Web access for nearly 10,000 users. They do all of this with only five FTEs providing support for the system.

Measurement and ROI

Measurement and ROI need to be based largely on the attention individuals within an organization give to the document or object being looked at for managing. Attention is the currency, so it should also be the unit of measure on which an organization's ROI is based. FileNet systems sometimes track every retrieval from a system, but most focus on knowing only what document types are retrieved regularly versus those archived only for regulatory compliance. Look for more-detailed ROI advice later in this book.

SUCCESS STORY

A worldwide provider of transportation services for B2B shippers of heavyweight cargo began to face tougher U.S. Customs laws. The company needed a replacement for its unwieldy image processing system. It required a more sophisticated Web-based system that could help customers process, manage, and track the enormous amount of customs paperwork required for every international shipment.

Using FileNet's ECM solution, the organization was able to couple a user-friendly interface with its existing system in less than six months. With the ability to automate the company's customs compliance workflow, the new combined system allowed documents that were created as part of the import process to be scanned or entered into the system at the point of origin and associated with existing customer data. The new system also enabled customers to use the Internet to view actual images of their customs documents, forecast import-related expenses, and create customs status reports.

The new system simplified compliance with U.S. Customs laws while giving customers Internet access to all relevant customs information, forms, and documentation. It also increased the speed with which customs clearances were processed for incoming goods.

Chapter 5

FILENET
INTEGRATION

All parts should go together without forcing. You must remember that the parts you are reassembling were disassembled by you. Therefore, if you can't get them together again, there must be a reason. By all means, do not use a hammer.

—IBM maintenance manual, 1925

KEY OBJECTIVES

■ Learn the advantages and disadvantages of implementing FileNet as a bolt-on application for larger systems.

■ Understand the basics of FileNet systems integration and what types of integration are available.

■ Know how to use a Web-browser interface to integrate a FileNet system with almost any other application.

■ Learn how to configure a Web farm to improve the availability of FileNet.

■ See how an imaging system like FileNet allows a company to improve the internal standardization of processes.

■ Gain a general knowledge of workflow tools, analysis, and documentation.

- Understand how metadata works as a context-based container and what opportunities and limitations this creates.
- Learn to recognize and avoid the common issues involved with capturing metadata effectively.
- Be aware of the litigation worries many have with capturing metadata.

Integrating Systems, Applications, and Processes

When looking at an integration project, a first determination to make is: What are the motives and objectives of this integration? At times, the stated motives and objectives are completely different; this causes many integration projects to be dysfunctional and often unsuccessful.

Effective systems integration is absolutely essential for maximum business efficiency and profitability. The information about your clients, products, inventory levels, sales, contacts, cash flow, accounts receivable, payables, employees, and your clients should be fully integrated. Once an organization has fully integrated its data, it can manage the data efficiently and leverage the data for increased profitability.

When trying to integrate an electronic document management system into an existing organization with decades of dependence on paper, the issue quickly becomes a trust issue. Can the computerized, paperless system be trusted to deliver the needed information accurately? Will all the paper documents be properly scanned and indexed? Should all relevant documents be printed, just to be safe?

If the leaders of an organization value their employees and are not just trying to downsize, they will quickly realize that these motives are important to their employees. A FileNet implementation has a greater chance for success if the employees currently responsible for the paper files are involved in the reengineering of the process. If the motive of the project is of job function growth and job routine diminishment, then employees should quickly be made to see their place in the organization is secure and growing in importance.

Integrating FileNet with Existing Systems

Often, an imaging system is seen as simply a bolt-on technology to increase the value of an existing system. Although this may work, it comes with its own set of issues. A FileNet system can "bolt on" extra functionality, but you could be limiting a very robust system built around disaster recovery and stability to handle a function already built into a lot of applications.

A second issue is the classic two-database problem. Adding a complete stand-alone system, which includes an index database, to an existing application that already has index records risks disagreement between the systems. An example is shown in Figure 5.1.

This scenario may offer advantages, such as load balancing for queries and fault tolerance. The price of these advantages is additional complexity. Handling a crashed database probably will require

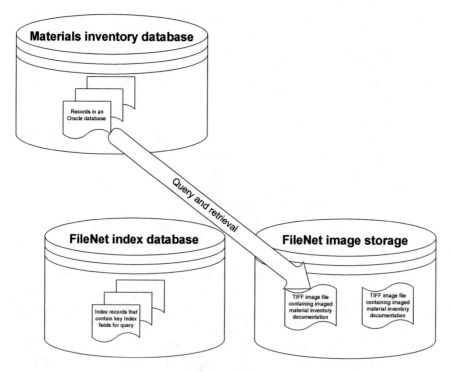

Figure 5.1
Dual database systems

a detection mechanism. Consistency is also an important aspect. All database instances must contain the same information, and regardless of which instance is queried, the result should be the same. This may require another component to ensure replication consistency.

Today, individuals and organizations build systems from a variety of diverse components. As the complexity of the technologies increases, more customers demand integrated solutions to their information issues. The increasingly large amount of hardware, software, and networking expertise companies are being forced to purchase has become unsustainable for many businesses.

This has led more and more IT organizations into becoming proponents of service-oriented architectures. They believe that the emerging technology of Web services will enable computer systems to discover a service on a network and connect to that service automatically without special programming. Some are even predicting that the high-paying systems integrators jobs of today may be completely automated in less than a decade.

APPLICATION INTEGRATION

Application integration is typically done in one of the following ways:

1. *Disintermediation.* A custom database application can be designed to accomplish all the tasks of the various software applications involved in the business process.
2. *Portal.* A centralized interface can be created to communicate, either directly or via open database connectivity (ODBC) interface, with each of the applications to manage the transfer of information.
3. *Data warehouse.* A centralized database can gather information from each of the programs to aggregate information and act as a reporting tool for the system as a whole.

FileNet's desktop client application currently offers integration with the following applications:

- Microsoft Office, including
  Word 97 and Word 2000
  Excel 97 and Excel 2000

Power Point 97 and PowerPoint 2000
Outlook 97, Outlook 98, and Outlook 2000
■ Lotus Notes 4.6.2a and above

Support for application integration allows access to special FileNet menu options that streamline document management functions within an interface on which users are already trained in. Some of the features supported by the integration are creating compound documents from within Office applications, viewing and modifying document and version properties, inserting document properties directly into Microsoft Word or Excel documents, and inserting documents and shortcuts in Outlook.

WEB INTEGRATION

As an alternative to the standard Panagon IDM Desktop client, FileNet offers a feature-rich Web client. The FileNet Web interface consists of a number of Component Object Model (COM) components stitched together with Active Server Pages code. It is not a thin client application, in the strictest sense of the term, as the viewing of TIFFs requires a plug-in software component for the browser. The FileNet Web viewer application integrates with the browser to allow it to display documents in over 200 different document formats.

The Web interface supports document retrieval, as well as other document management (DM) features, like check-in, check-out, version control, annotation creation, and even the ability to create new documents and save them into the repository. Unfortunately, the Web client lacks some of the search features available in the thick client version, is not as easily integrated with desktop applications, and requires the user to perform more steps to add documents to the repository. It is important to note that, since it allows specific documents to be referenced via hyperlinks, the Web interface can facilitate integration with almost any software.

As an alternative to FileNet's Web interface, companies can build their own custom Web interface on IBM's WebSphere platform using a "resource adapter" that FileNet has created, called ISRA. It is a system-level software driver, compliant with the J2EE Connector Architecture v1.0. The ISRA can be used by a JAVA application component or client to connect to FileNet Image Services via a browser interface.

The server side of the FileNet Web integration is FileNet Web Services, which can be operated on a Microsoft 2000 platform. The Web server has all of the typical functionality of a Web server and can be coupled with an organization's ERP implementation to provide Web-based access to ERP and image information. Figure 5.2 is an overview of an ERP environment's integration with a single FileNet Web server.

In the figure, starting in the upper left corner, are two FileNet Capture clients, a scanner and an indexer, both directly linking to the UNIX server via a client server connection. The FileNet UNIX server stores the images of captured invoice documents for the approval process. Accounts payables invoice approvers access the SAP UNIX server via a client server connection and work the invoices in their SAP inbox. If they need to view an invoice, SAP provides a URL with the appropriate FileNet document ID to the invoice approver's browser. The URL and ID launch FileNet and provide a security authentication screen for login. After login, the image is displayed.

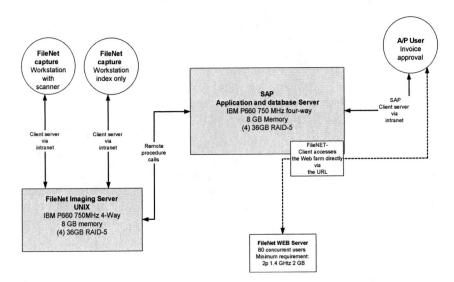

Figure 5.2
SAP integration on a single FileNet Web server

Viewing TIFFs requires the downloading of a TIFF viewer because a multipage TIFF viewer is not built into the Web browser. FileNet provides a TIFF viewer that can be set up to download the first time an end user hits the site to retrieve an image. If your organization is rolling out this technology to a large population for the first time, it is usually advisable to push the viewer installation out to the entire population instead of waiting for the first time each logs in.

Figure 5.3 is the same basic FileNet ERP solution with additional emphasis on FileNet's Web retrieval. A properly configured NT Web server supports around 80 concurrent users. As the usage level of 80 concurrent users begins to be reached, it is normally a good idea to remove the single point of failure of the one FileNet Web server.

Multiple FileNet Web servers can be set up to work as a multi-server "Web farm" when combined with Cisco's Redirector (load

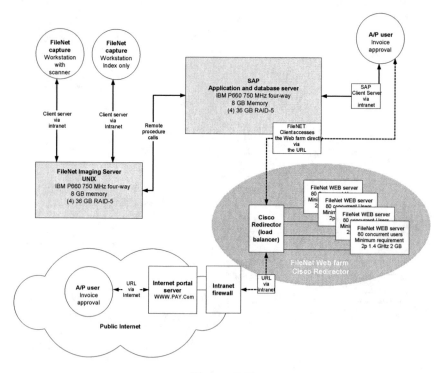

Figure 5.3
SAP Integration/Cisco FileNet Web farm

balancer). The Redirector is like a router that continuously polls the FileNet Web servers to determine if they are operational and balances the load of incoming image requests. The Cisco Redirector uses a virtual IP address and name to combine access to all four servers into a single IP address and name.

In addition to the ability to handle the increased concurrent users that the Web farm adds, the Redirector can also be used in an Internet-facing architecture. The figure shows how the director can be used with a firewall and a portal server to allow Internet users to log in and access images via the Net.

ENTERPRISE RESOURCE PLANNING INTEGRATION

FileNet has used standardization of processes, procedures, and technology to integrate with enterprise resource planning systems such as SAP and PeopleSoft. This standardization has allowed FileNet to become a satellite product that can be implemented along with most ERP systems.

Eli Whitney is best known for his invention of the cotton gin, but another great feat of his was to completely reinvent the America manufacturing process by introducing interchangeable parts and mass production. Until this point, items were made one at a time, but Whitney wanted to make high-quality items easier and faster.

His first project was the manufacture of muskets. After gaining a contract from the government, he set out to make 2000 guns in two years. Although he did not meet his goal until 10 years later, the changes he made to the production process allowed him to make 10,000 guns in two years. The two major innovations in this process were the standardized parts and the milling machine.

The standardization of parts allowed them to be cut from a pattern that even a relatively unskilled worker could retrace. It made the parts virtually interchangeable, allowing huge process simplifications. These process simplifications reduced waste, time, and materials as well as reducing the training time required to bring in new workers.

Most ERP systems implementations require the standardization of business processes to match the system modules. Although this standardization is difficult during the first implementation, following upgrades are quick and relatively inexpensive because of the standardized processes and modules. The process improvements this type of standardization enables are substantial. An imaging system like FileNet allows you to bring this standardization of processes to your document handling.

FileNet's imaging products are designed to compliment a wide variety of enterprise systems. One of the biggest uses of FileNet is to provide imaging or document management functionality as a "bolt-on" to existing ERP platforms. Typically, integration with FileNet is provided via one or more of three routes:

1. FileNet middleware products such as ClientLink for SAP integration or PeopleLink for Peoplesoft integration.
2. Custom applications utilizing the various FileNet toolkits and resource adapters.
3. Third-party portals and workflow engines such as Fuegoware.

When the system integration is done right, most users do not even know they are using FileNet. It simply appears as if every needed document is stored right in the ERP system. In addition to the ROI provided by imaging itself, this allows the most basic business processes to be enhanced through workflow applications.

Workflow applications manage the flow and routing of work within a process or group of processes. Utilizing the highest degree of automation possible, workflow applications can assemble information, dispatch it to the correct persons, monitor and report on progress, set and reset priorities in the order of work, and even assist in estimating future needs.

Some of the main benefits of using workflow technology include:

- *Accountability*: Increased integrity and reliability of processes through clearly defined rules and actively monitored audit trails.
- *Shorter processing cycles*: Reduction of task time through automation and routing.
- *Increased communication*: Automatic sharing of critical information, avoiding the bottlenecks that often appear as processes that cross the lines separating departments.
- *Improved metrics*: Automatic monitoring of performance and workflow statistics so metrics are more available and less subjective, which leads to better decision making.

■ *Better customer service*: Shorter process time, faster access, and improved accuracy so response to customers is much more efficient; removing feedback delays improves almost any system.

Workflow Analysis

Workflow analysis is a process information managers can use to examine how the work gets done in that operation and to identify opportunities for improvement. It is also an effective first step in automating library and information center processes and making new technology choices. All business processes have a workflow, but not all workflows need enterprise-level workflow technology. When best practices are understood and systemized, they drive the financial success of the business, no matter what tools you use.

Achieving the optimum workflow requires a thorough understanding of the business's goals, in-depth analysis of the current workflow, and a strategic plan for changing old systems or implementing new systems. This all begins with conducting a thorough workflow analysis. Be very cautious about outsourcing this task, as it will play a major role in determining the scope of future technology purchases.

Workflow Analysis Steps

1. Define the scope of the project.
2. Gather and list business processes.
3. Create process definitions and workflow diagrams.
4. Define as-is workflow specification and identify the following:
   ■ Points in the workflow where critical decisions are made.
   ■ Stages in the workflow that require the collaborative effort of multiple workers.
   ■ Specific employee and computing resources applied during each stage.
   ■ Specific applications, external resources, databases, and people required at each stage.
5. Identify objectives for improvement: Typical objectives include improving accountability, speed, cost, scalability, disaster recovery, headcount reduction, and risk management.

6. Define to-be workflow specification:
   - Choose whether to use a message-oriented or repository-oriented workflow architecture (although message-oriented systems are usually cheaper and quicker to put in place, repository-based systems usually offer better reporting options).
   - Identify opportunities to improve quality, reduce rework, ramp up performance, and reduce duplication of effort.
7. Document Functional Requirements:
   - Performance requirements.
   - Security requirements.
   - Quality requirements.
8. Define monitoring and reporting specifications:
   - Consider metrics for monitoring data capture worker performance.
   - Establish system performance benchmarks and monitoring metrics (OSAR versus cache retrieval ratios, concurrent user counts, system uptime, and so on).
   - Identify strategic business process planning and reporting metrics (average invoice amount, average time-to-pay, expense overruns by department, and so on).

Workflow Diagrams

Workflow diagrams help a company standardize processes and identify critical paths that provide progress and performance measurement. The clearer and more standardized the process is, the more likely quality will be consistently high. However, if the workflow process stifles dialog and innovation you may end up sacrificing long-term sustainability for near-term gains.

Focusing on the process of implementing projects can increase the efficiency with which projects are planned and executed, but the information and knowledge must be shared.

Figure 5.4 demonstrates that, on future executions, the "distance delay" is reduced through the integration of KM principles and the overall project efficiency is increased. The more often humans do something according to a formal process, the more efficient they typically become. This is well known in sports, so coaches push training. It is well known in manufacturing, so companies push assembly

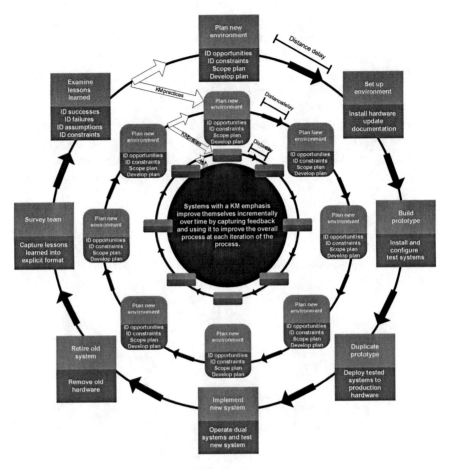

Figure 5.4
KM-focused circular business process example

lines and prefabrication. Why is this type of repetitiveness not driven into project management? It is in well-managed organizations.

Workflow diagrams provide an excellent tool for documenting many types of projects. Examples include analyzing as-is and to-be scenarios, designing new process flows, documenting procedures, and supporting business process reengineering. They represent the dynamics of a system by expressing the flow of events and are an ideal way to help visualize the workflow of a system. Describing complex procedures using text alone can yield lengthy documents that allow conflicting interpretations by reviewers. The results or solutions depicted by workflow diagrams help determine if automation can enhance or support an activity.

Diagrams of enterprise workflows often employ cross-functional flowcharts, also known as *swim-lane diagrams* (see Figure 5.5). Swim-lane diagrams are helpful tools when modeling business workflows because they can show how some procedures integrate organizational units within a business model. Such a workflow analysis separates the process diagram into parallel segments, called *swim lanes*. Each swim lane shows a department or role and contains the

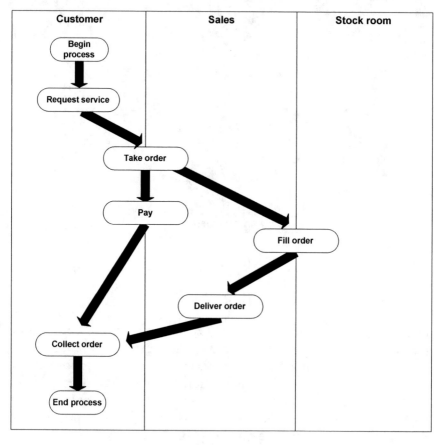

Figure 5.5
Swim lane diagram of simple sales process

activities of that role. Transitions can take place from one swim lane to another. Unlike system diagrams that emphasize the flow of control between objects, swim-lane diagrams emphasize the flow of control between activities, events, groups, and individuals.

The old adage that a picture is worth a thousand words is especially true with workflow diagrams. Achieving the optimum workflow depends on developing a thorough understanding of the business's goals, an in-depth analysis of the current workflow, and a strategic plan for implementing new systems or bolstering existing systems.

To be successful, the needs of *all* the stakeholder groups must be taken into account. This begins with conducting a thorough workflow analysis. Carefully examine the points where process tasks switch swim lanes, as these are often the problem points in a workflow. Be very cautious about outsourcing this task, as it often determines the scope of technology purchases.

INTEGRATIONS AND METADATA

All the integration scenarios in this chapter have at least one thing in common—metadata. In the information technology world, *meta* is a prefix that means "an underlying definition or description." In relation to data and information, it means "more comprehensive or fundamental." *Metadata* is a description of content; it is data that describes other data. Naturally, different users may see different descriptions and the fundamental way of defining the content.

Various types of metadata have been developed to support information management needs. Metadata for record keeping orders, validates and archives an organization's records. Preservation metadata contributes to the long-term retention of resources. Descriptive metadata are used for identification, discovery and access, and evaluation of resources. All types of metadata support the management of resources to ensure access to them both now and for the entire life cycle of the content.

Within enterprise content management systems, metadata describes every object of content, and the metadata that facilitates easy content retrieval. The integration of any two databases depends on identifying key fields that bind them together. This relationship between systems can be created using the metadata.

To bind an SAP record with a FileNet invoice image, merely capture the FileNet document ID number into a field of the SAP record. Another option would be to include the SAP record number into the metadata for the FileNet invoice image. Most users choose to include the FileNet document ID number into the SAP record. This is because FileNet provides workflow tools to capture the number into the SAP record when it is scanned. FileNet also provides a utility to allow retrieving the image from the FileNet repository by selecting a button in the SAP interface.

Metadata is like a container for a document, and all containers are both facilitators and limiters. A farmer that grows corn may find that canning the corn facilitates some markets for this product. However, the container also limits the market for his corn at the same time. The livestock feed and corn-on-the-cob customers are bound to be disappointed. Containers like metadata both facilitate and limit the use of information, because when the metadata is defined loosely it limits retrievals and when it is defined too strictly it limits reuse.

Imaging System Metadata Issues

Imaging systems are focused on rapid retrievals of static documents: Their key features are simple interfaces, quick retrievals, and high availability from any location. Metadata is typically added to a document image when the document is scanned. Future changes in metadata are usually contained in annotations. These systems usually drive very mature business processes, so the documents captured benefit from long-established categorization practices.

The maturity of the business processes that traditional imaging systems support make the retrieval needs much more predictable than in more-dynamic electronic document management systems. The wise project manager spends a good deal of planning time analyzing and documenting the way the end users query for images. In a traditional imaging system, rapid retrieval from a simple interface, using one or two key metadata fields is much more important than advanced query interfaces and keyword searches. Knowledge management and electronic document management functions usually require more advanced query screens and keyword searching.

Unfortunately, metadata occasionally are missing or incorrect because the data entry clerk (or optical character recognition engine) was sloppy, poorly trained, or both. In these types of systems, the viewers of the documents are rarely empowered to change the metadata associated with them. However, they are usually the first ones to spot the inevitable indexing mistakes that occurred. To provide strong exception handling, the issues need to be considered early in any imaging project.

This makes it valuable to set up an easy-to-use, rapid feedback system for users to report metadata problems. With a Web-based system, it is pretty easy to script a function to e-mail an indexing error notification back to the data capture department. Called from a button on the Web-viewing interface, it should send the FileNET document ID number along with the date and e-mail address of the user that observed the problem.

Electronic Content Management Metadata Issues

Electronic content management systems focus on encouraging collaboration and making valuable intellectual assets easily located and reused. They manage content objects that are dynamic rather than of fixed content, like imaging systems. Most of these systems rely on document authors to assign the metadata to describe the context of the documents. This usually does not work particularly well. The purposes of documents like Word documents and PowerPoint presentations are better defined by other people's use and opinion of them than by the somewhat limited and biased opinions of authors. A main rule of content management is this: For metadata to be useful, it has to be honest.

In the late 1990s, this was demonstrated with Web documents via the "meta keywords" tag for Internet documents. The meta keywords tag was created as a way to insert a context description (metadata) into an HTML page. The meta tag is not visible when the page is viewed through a browser, but search engines could read the content of the tag and use the words in it, along with the page's regular body copy, to provide results for user queries. Sadly, within a year, most Internet analysts declared the keywords meta tag useless. The tag had almost immediately become unreliable because authors tried to promote their works with insincere meta tags. After all, it is an attention-based economy, and Web-page hits are valuable.

What is needed for EDM systems, knowledge bases, intellectual asset archives, and the like is a system that generates highly reliable sources of whatever kind of information is asked for, based on the search terms provided. For success stories, look to Internet search engine leader Google and bookseller Amazon.com. Both depend on highly sophisticated ranking and review systems to ensure the quality of their metadata archives. They figured out that the key metadata for their systems are based on managing reputations, relationships, and links—the key assets in an economy based on attention.

Google WebSearch™ calls its ranking system for metadata PageRank™. It typically generates highly reliable sources for most kinds of information you might ask for. PageRank's intelligent algorithm allows it to evaluate the context and credibility of Web pages based on the quality and amount of links between the page itself and other documents. However, even with Google's highly sophisticated system, it is still difficult to research "spanking" in the context of corporal punishment and avoid seeing a mountain of pornography sites.

Google does not even bother reading the meta tags the author assigned to the content. It merely reads the document's relationship with other documents on the same subject and uses that information to figure out how respected is the information or information provider. The strategy has been so successful that many people cannot imagine a day when they are not using Google for something.

Legal Metadata Issues

Today, many lawyers are beginning to focus on the issue of the document properties, metadata carried by documents, particularly those generated by Microsoft products. Such metadata includes information contained in prior drafts, comments, information about authors and sources, and other items that can result in embarrassing and damaging disclosures for clients and law firms alike.

Comments can contain text that may be inappropriate to share. People sometimes use language during document creation that they would never want in the final version. To address issues like these, several firms are attacking the problem by using software tools to scrub out all the metadata in their Microsoft Office documents. In most cases however, these solutions have addressed solely Microsoft Word documents.

Whatever the objectives of your metadata strategy, you will benefit from careful planning and dialog among the stakeholders. The metadata choices made during implementation of a content management system have a huge impact on the systems future effectiveness, performance, and ability to integrate.

Success Story

A worldwide organization operating in more than 25 counties needed a more effective way for individuals with organizational accounts receivable responsibilities to query and access A/R information. The existing system was paper based, with entries being completed manually in an Oracle database system. The FileNet solution implemented took advantage of FileNet's thin client and used Web technology to distribute purchase orders, invoices, and checks to customers.

This implementation included the ability to allow authorized employees to view, print, and fax invoices or purchase orders data via the Internet.

The system resulted a reduction in the cost of receivables by nearly 50%. Other customer benefits included better resolution of billing questions and payment disputes, normally during the customer's call. Fewer delays naturally created happier customers—and more sales.

Chapter 6

FileNet Administration

Leadership is getting someone to do what they don't want to do,
to achieve what they want to achieve.

—Tom Landry

Key Objectives

- Seasoned system administrators develop special knowledge and experience from continuously monitoring and maintaining their systems. Capturing and distributing this knowledge is important when planning upgrades and vital when planning installation and integration projects.
- Learn techniques for managing technicians and administrators with extremely introverted personalities and underdeveloped communication skills.
- Understand the basic tasks of the average FileNet system administrator and the new regulatory issues created by HIPAA and the Sarbanes-Oxley Act of 2002.
- Know where to go and what questions to ask to gather the critical data needed to implement and administrate an enterprise imaging system.

100

- Become familiar with the key UNIX-based administrative tools for maintaining a FileNet system and keeping it running efficiently.
- Learn how to build FileNet systems that focus on supporting transaction-processing or record-keeping goals.
- See multiple examples of FileNet system architectures to support centralized or decentralized data capture operations.
- Learn what typical installation and client-side support issues to expect with a large-scale FileNet project.

Profiting from Your Organization's Experience

Administrators can be key content and dialog contributors because of their experience continuously maintaining systems. Most administrators deal with implementing integrations with a number of new systems regularly. Maintaining highly integrated system equipment often requires developing clever ways of maintaining uptime, facilitating the replacement of hardware, patching operating systems (OS), and upgrading applications. Because of the variety of work that administrators do, they often know (and are willing to admit) more about the actual operation of a system than the vendor that provided it. This knowledge is important when planning upgrades and vital when looking at integration projects.

Although administrators have a lot of vital knowledge, getting it out of them can be a challenge. Often administrators have held their positions for years, and sharing knowledge is looked on as giving away the job. Many technical administrators also have introverted personalities and underdeveloped communication skills. Building trust with these communities requires time and effort. It is helpful to begin developing that trust before the input is needed.

Often, those that administrate a system and those that build improvements to a system are in different business groups, with competing goals that can build pressure between the groups. This is not uncommon, but it poses an issue that drains the attention of both groups and can create strife. To avoid this, the two groups should be brought together to participate in activities outside the direct work environment. One of the best examples of this type of activity is a corporate "ropes" program.

The ropes course is a highly interactive, energetic program designed to create individual and work group growth experience. It aids building a sense of interdependence and shared vision that facilitates working together as a high-performance team. The alien environment and high ropes challenges involved are 30–50 feet off the ground and require team members to pull together, support, and coach one another. The participants learn to trust and cooperate to get through the many physical and psychological challenges offered.

No one is forced or coerced to participate; each individual can choose how much challenge is right for him or her. Individuals and teams experience the positive feelings that overcoming each ropes course challenges bring, and no two groups experience the ropes course in the same way.

Another way to help build these relationships is to create a rewards program that allows employees to recognize their coworkers for exceptional efforts. At IBM, employees are encouraged to reward other workers within "Big Blue" that excel in supporting them. They personalized their program by providing a number of IBM-logo-bearing shirts, pens, and other small niceties for rewards and an online system to track usage and rules compliance. Since all the gift items carry the company logo, they are also building the IBM brand, while building better relationships.

FILENET ADMINISTRATOR DUTIES

FileNet systems are engineered to require a small number of administrative support personnel relative to the size of the user base. Due to the wide range of potential infrastructure configurations, integration choices, and customer-programmed enhancements, administrating FileNet systems and its customizable applications can require specialized expertise. The local FileNet system administrator is a critical component of a enterprise content management system, because of the number of users who rely on the system being up and running. In this chapter, we examine the administration needs, expectations, and resources available for FileNet.

Most FileNet support teams are light in the system administrative area, compared to their FileNet client-side support and development teams. This typically is no problem because of the stability of FileNet. Another reason that FileNet systems can be operated with fewer administrators is that you can always hire FileNet to administrate your system to cover periods in which support is limited or nonexistent due to such things as emergencies, vacations, extended illnesses, or employee attrition. However, that solution should be seen as a last resort.

A FileNet administrator generally handles the following tasks:

■ Security and backup.
■ Optical storage and retrieval maintenance.
■ Document class setup.
■ System monitoring and diagnostics.
■ Images services server monitoring and maintenance.
■ FileNet Web servers.
■ Oracle database maintenance.
■ System upgrades.
■ Configuration changes.
■ Data migration.

Sarbanes-Oxley Act of 2002

Administrators of FileNet systems must be aware of the critical nature of the data and processes they use and preserve. The Sarbanes-Oxley Act of 2002 requires senior management to be *personally* responsible for the information and processes by which their organization reports financial information. This means that enterprise content management is more important than ever before. It also means that administrators need to monitor their systems and processes closely to avoid costly oversights.

The top 10 warning signs of potential Sarbanes-Oxley risk are these:

1. A records-management policy not linked to regulatory requirements.
2. Retention schedules disconnected from legal department policies.
3. Formal document handling policies nonexistent or inconsistent across departments.
4. A records management policy that covers only paper documents.

5. Document management systems that have no clearly identified individuals responsible for assuring their continuing regulatory compliance.
6. Document retention periods that are not integrated with enterprise content management to purge both digital and analog documents.
7. Records-management policies not communicated to employees.
8. Lack of processes and tools to authorize deleting documents.
9. No auditing of the entire records-management process.
10. Documents and content without metadata, preventing the retrieval of required documents.

Gathering Critical System Planning Data

Often, the administrators are put on implementation teams as organizations face expanding their FileNet systems. This means that administrators are often expected to be experts on system installation, when the majority of their experience may strictly be administration and security. To help with these issues, this section lays out some common tasks and questions to perform to ease the learning curve.

This section is intended for FileNet IM (Image Manager) administrators and network planning personnel. It assumes that the reader has a basic understanding of networks, an understanding of planning and configuration issues associated with networks, and a strong working knowledge of the FileNet IM product line. Attending FileNet's administration training classes helps in the planning process but cannot replace genuine field experience.

The first step in planning an IM system is to gather information about the documents and processes for the in-scope area of the organization. An effective way to gather the needed information is by conducting interviews with representatives from each identifiable business process. While this may seem time consuming, it has proven to be one of the best ways to consolidate and organize the details necessary for a successful IM implementation.

The goal is to gather information about the nature and flow of information and documents within the organization. This helps identify the necessary resources for the design of the IM system to meet the business's specific needs. If the time has not been taken to gather this information before beginning an implement, often the result is a second project to fix the issues generated by the implementation. This type of rework is shockingly expensive.

It is important to gather organizational information to help with the decisions referring to the overall system configuration. This information includes items such as budgetary constraints that could affect the design of the system. It is also important to collect information that affects the index structures and metadata. Along with this information, it is important to understand the project's stakeholder structure and design forms or interfaces for collecting security information for users.

The following list is a good place to start to gather stakeholder information: division heads, department heads, administrative assistants, work processing managers, delivery and document handling personnel, and network administrators (WAN and LAN).

What types of WANs, LANs, servers, and client machines are used, and what is the available bandwidth? This is important to answer because a system implementation falls flat on its face if it causes network issues. If the interviews are performed well and detailed information is gathered and analyzed, the overall structure and requirements should begin to follow into place. As you interview your sources, ask the following questions:

- What is the network setup?
- Are DNS servers or host files being used for domain name resolution?
- What types of documents will be in the system, and what are their requirements?
- Where documents are to be stored and accessed?
- What are the hardware and software requirements?
- Is an existing system diagram available?
- What custom metadata properties are needed?
- Will the FileNet system require multiple document classes? (Refer to Chapter 3 for more information on document classes and families.)
- Who will access each document class?
- How do the individual groups communicate to work together? (Please list departments, project teams, and functional or cross-functional work groups.)

- What security rights are needed, for both groups and individuals and for each document class? (Refer to Chapter 3 for more information on document classes and families.)
- What is the expectation for image retrieval speed and system uptime?
- What needs to be added, if anything, to the current network infrastructure to support a FileNet system at the desired performance level?
- Do any of the servers or network components require upgrading to meet the project goals?
- Does any existing client software need upgrading; if so, to how many users?
- Are the system diagrams, network information, and LAN/WAN description documents up to date?

FileNet system configuration and performance depend on the network as well as the client and server hardware and software configuration. It is critical to have an updated network topology diagram that describes your network and a detailed system diagram to show where integration points occur.

The following are general FileNet project questions:

- Total number of current documents and pages?
- Average number of new documents and pages added daily?
- Average number of annotations added to a document?
- List of the primary index keys?
- How many of the index fields are to be autoindexed?
- How many documents are expected to be captured by the end of first year?
- What is the estimated initial repository size?
- How much BES cache should be assigned?
- How much Page cache should be assigned?
- How much total disk storage space is required?

Assemble the following server information:

- Server location: Physical location, including building address.
- Server name: Full server name, including alias.
- Operating system: Type of OS and version (example, AIX 4.3.3).
- Database: Type and version.
- Memory: Total installed and available.

- Disk space: Total installed and available after partitioning and redundancy.
- Replication: Type of mirroring being used.

Each group has its own security template defined for viewing and manipulating documents stored in the FileNet system. Discussions with the project team members give a better understanding of security policies and requirements. Keep in mind that administrators, as a group, have full rights to all documents in the document library. Only system administration staff members should belong to the administrators group.

When requesting security information from the project team, be very specific from the first as to the information that you need. A good place to start is with the following: project name, user ID, full name, e-mail address, mirror ID (existing user name that can be used as a template, helpful if the requesting person does not understand the document class structure).

A number of possible access levels could be given to a group or individual. We hope these examples give a clearer understanding of the levels of security that can be assigned, at the user account level, to each document class:

- *Admin*: Owner access rights plus the ability to modify all property values.
- *Owner*: Author access rights plus the ability to modify most property values, including security, and to delete the document.
- *Author*: Viewer access rights plus the ability to check out and check in the document and change a few property values.
- *Viewer*: The ability to view, annotate, and make copies of the document and view the properties.
- *None*: No access; the user cannot even verify that the object exists in the system.

UNIX Administrative Tools and Resources

- The FileNet *Task Manager* application allows you to control and monitor the FileNet software. Launch Task Manager by entering the UNIX command: Xtaskman. The program can be run in the background to allow the starting and stopping of the

FileNet software, the monitoring of process, and the preparation of EBR (FileNet's UNIX-based Enterprise Systems Backup utility) backups and restorations.

- The *SEC_tool* is a command-line-driven utility for managing licensing and security account information. From here, you can see who is logged in and unlock any accounts locked-out due to excessive concurrent login attempts.
- *fn_util* is a command-line-driven program that allows administrators to start, stop, update, or initialize FileNet databases. *Warning*: Use this program with extreme caution; used incorrectly, it can destroy all your index data.
- *fn_edit* is the configuration editor for FileNet imaging systems, another command-line-driven program. Using fn_edit allows administrators to edit a long list of configuration values on the server, such as:

Network addresses	Performance tuning
System attributes	Storage libraries
System defaults	Peer systems
Application services	Procedures
Relational databases	Printing
MKF_databases	Server attributes

- The Xapex command in UNIX initiates the FileNet *Application Executive* program, which serves as the primary administration tool for FileNet imaging systems. From the Application Executive's GUI interface, an administrator can perform a wide range of tasks, such as:
  - Create or modify the system database structure.
  - Create accounts or modify security settings for individuals or groups.
  - Perform cache backups and audit security.
  - Monitor the storage library and system statistics.
  - Initiate background jobs, such as importing documents, consolidating media, and migrating documents to new storage media.

Typical FileNet System Structure

The majority of FileNet root servers operate on the AIX UNIX operating system; however, the SUN UNIX has been gaining ground and some organizations even use Windows servers for their FileNet root servers. The majority of the peripheral systems operate on Microsoft Windows 2000. They are usually put into place to support highly visible enterprise transaction processing systems.

Transaction processing systems are the most common business systems. Like most large enterprise software packages, the basic design is intended to separate the functions of input, processing, and output. Although this is also true for enterprise-level record-keeping applications, there are also differences to consider. For example, although you can use a transaction processing system for record keeping, it was built with very different goals.

Transaction processing systems are centered on using current data, saved in the most efficient manner possible with a strong focus on performance. Record-keeping systems like FileNet are focused more on consistency, sustainability, and the long-term availability of information. In a transaction system, record keeping may be a by-product of the business process, but it is not the primary purpose of the system.

There are a variety of secondary services for FileNet and countless ways to configure the system. Figure 6.1 shows a sample architectural plan for a typical FileNet configuration. The AIX UNIX operating system is used for the production and development root servers, but the peripheral servers use the Windows NT operating system. The Windows NT operating system can be used for small production root servers, but it is not widely considered to be as scalable as UNIX operating system based implementations.

The Web farm shown in the figure should handle between 300 and 400 concurrent users and offers intelligent server farm load balancing provided by a product called Cisco Local Director™. For more redundancy you can add additional Cisco directors and more Web servers to increase stability. For a general idea of concurrent users versus the total FileNet population, we look to an accounts payable example.

A large oil company has approximately 10,000 FileNet users that approve invoices throughout the month. The normal peak usage during a given week is 300–400 concurrent users, giving an approximate factor of 1 concurrent user to 29 user accounts.

Figure 6.2 shows a similar architecture that includes components to support remote data capture (scanning and indexing from a remote site). The figure is a high level example of FileNet server components

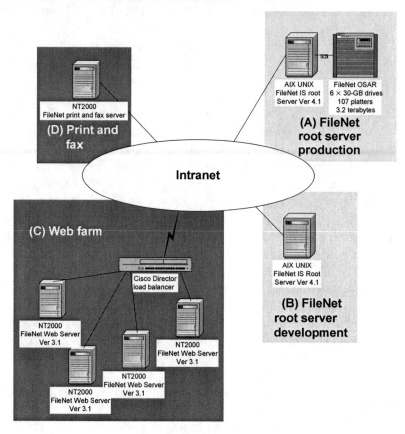

Figure 6.1

Typical FileNet system configuration

being used in an environment where the data capture (scanning and indexing) is handled at a distant location or outsourced to a capture vendor.

Using business transformation outsourcing (BTO) providers is becoming more common as the drive to decentralize and move business components offshore increases. Business transformation outsourcing is similar to business process outsourcing (BPO) but typically includes additional improvements to existing processes that the purchasing company could not (or would not) implement while

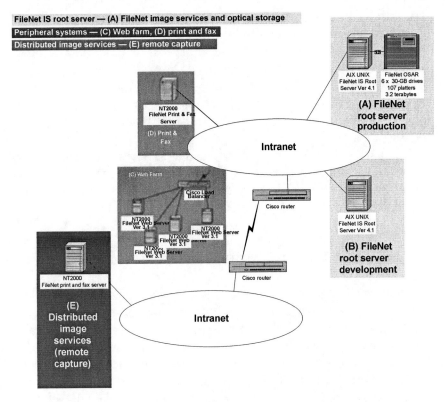

Figure 6.2
Typical FileNet system configuration with remote capture

the task was being performed in-house. Distributed Image Services is a name FileNet often uses to describe certain image services components that are replicated at remote locations.

In Figure 6.2, both the Batch Entry Services cache and the Page cache would be replicated on the DIS server. This would enable localized caching of images for quick retrieval and the localized caching of scanned images and index batches awaiting committal to the optical storage and retrieval system. FileNet's IM software can be configured to automatically maintain replication consistency between its internal BES and Page caches and the external distributed image services' BES and Page caches.

Keep in mind, when looking at remote capture opportunities, that, although the DIS server has images cached, it does not provide replication of the security database. The security database for an IM resides on the root server (main FileNet imaging system server). If the root server is down, the DIS server is inaccessible, because users cannot log in to FileNet's security.

If an installation requires distributed security, then a second image services server (and license) is required. FileNet's IM can then be configured to use replication to maintain consistency between the two security databases.

Other names for the distributed image services are *remote entry server*, *batch entry services*, and *application server*. Again, please note that these are very high-level overviews and describe only a fraction of the ways that FileNet's products can be deployed.

Client Installation and Administration

An organization that is building a FileNet imaging application can expect that more than half of its administrator hours to be consumed by user support. In addition to the support issues there are ongoing upgrade path, as well as customer satisfaction issues to overcome. Project managers need a good understanding of the project's technical and political complexities to enable them to set the proper expectation when choosing a client type. One example is the FileNet client software. FileNet offers a thick client and a thin client. Because of the nature of imaging applications, imaging-thick clients can be difficult to configure and distribute over a large network.

In an SAP installation, SAP defines the procedures and specifications required to access SAP information and provide tight integration with the imaging vendor's product. FileNet's product line for this standard is named ClientLink for R3™.

Depending on the SAP client installation, several thick and thin configuration options are available for integrating SAP and FileNet. Figure 6.3 shows an example of a thick client installation on a user's workstation. The figure shows the FileNet software being delivered via an automated software push. Note the order in which the software is pushed is important: If it is not pushed in the correct order, the installation may not work (thick client first, middleware second).

Another installation item to keep in mind is that SMS pushes of the SAP GUI updates have been known to corrupt the existing installation of the FileNet client. For this reason, any time an SAP GUI

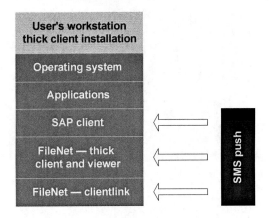

Figure 6.3
FileNet thick client installation

software push is taking place, it is important to test it against an existing workstation containing a FileNet installation of the thick client and Clientlink for R3. If the FileNet client is corrupted, a re-push of FileNet normally corrects the problem.

Thick client installations are typically more difficult to maintain because patches or upgrades require packaging and scheduling for SMS pushes. Moving to a thin client installation, however, more than likely will not reduce the overall support costs. The main reason for this is that, although client costs may be reduced, there is an increase in the total number of NT servers that must be supported. FileNet resources are typically more expensive than NT resources and can be difficult to find; therefore, it may be more cost effective to have a larger number of NT servers to support than trying to recruit more FileNet technical personnel resources.

Figure 6.4 shows an end-user's workstation and the FileNet software installed on it, including an example of where the software can be loaded. The only application, from a FileNet perspective, that needs to reside on the end-user's desktop in a "thin client installation" is the FileNet viewer. Web browsers do not natively view TIFF images; therefore, FileNet provides a viewer that views TIFFs and approximately 200 other formats. *Note*: FileNet's Panagon Document Warehouse version 5.1 provides a thin client that uses a Java applet downloaded for every viewing session.

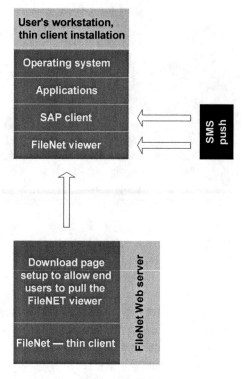

Figure 6.4
FileNet thin client installation

Multiple options are available for installing the FileNet thin client viewer software. One option is to push the viewer to the desktop through an SMS push, another is to allow the end user to pull the viewer to the desktop. Both options have strong points and drawbacks. A combination of the two may provide the best opportunity for success.

The main drawback of the SMS push method is the time required for the user to receive the push and start using the software. The drawback with the user pulling the viewer from the FileNet Web server is the problems that often arise from tasking individuals with installing their own software. Often this is no option because the end user lacks administrative rights to his or her desktop. Therefore, combining the two options may offer the best solution for many organizations.

As a FileNet implementation project nears completion, an SMS push can handle pushing the TIFF viewer to the FileNet thin-client users. Once the project is completed and for users that were not set up as part of the implementation need access, administration has the option of pushing new users the TIFF viewer through SMS or allowing the user to pull it from the FileNet Web server. This combined approach may offer the best of both worlds.

When a user accesses the FileNet Web interface home page for the first time, FileNet's standard interface has built-in code that examines the user's workstation to determine whether or not it has the viewer already installed. If the viewer is not installed, the interface offers to install it at that time. Expect some users to have problems with their installations, usually due to not exiting out of running programs before installing software. This is almost always an issue with self-service software installations, but it is usually manageable.

SUCCESS STORY

A European online brokerage that operates one of the most successful Web businesses in Germany was looking to reduce mailing costs. The company recently had seen explosive growth because of its drive to use innovative technology and leadership to maintain its competitive position. As with any corporate growth cycle, this one generated a large amount of documents.

The firm mails millions of confirmations, statements, and other paper documents each month. To reduce costs and improve customer satisfaction, the firm again looks to implement innovative technology. The firm focuses on offering online customer access to statements, order information, and cancellations. Another requirement of the system is to manage the electronic storage of documents in accordance with newly expanding government regulations.

The solution the brokerage company chooses includes a FileNet ECM system, because of its scalability, security, Web client availability, and ability to accommodate heavy traffic. The brokerage company's customers now have online informational archives to replace the mailed documents. The solution not only reduces the firm's administrative costs but also increases customer satisfaction immensely.

Summary of Benefits

- Reduced administrative costs through the elimination of costs associated with mailing paper information to customer base.
- Improved customer service through faster responses and greater levels of transparency.
- Process improvements that mean savings for the customers and increased transparency that improves customer trust.
- Online access to trade and customer documentation via the Web, which saves distribution costs and hassles.
- Meeting government regulatory requirements to avoid fines and costly litigation.

Chapter 7

FileNet and Knowledge Management

In organizations, real power and energy is generated through relationships. The patterns of relationships and the capacities to form them are more important than tasks, functions, roles, and positions.

—Margaret Wheatley

Key Objectives

- Learn how content management systems help facilitate the creation of new knowledge.
- Understand some ways that document management and imaging systems can support high-level KM initiatives.
- Know what differentiates imaging from other forms of content management.
- Learn the four most common methods of managing unstructured data and information while increasing actionable knowledge within an organization.
- Understand the value of finding common ground through mutually shared abstractions.

117

- Recognize that actionable knowledge leads to innovation only in the presence of both attention and retention by peers.
- Learn to use balanced scorecard documents to monitor and improve a group's performance.
- Know how document management processes can be evolved to maximize the three kinds of attention: awareness, reaction, and reflection.
- Understand how workflow can be used to add context to unstructured data.

Knowledge Management, Culture, and Content

Linking documents and content to people may be the single most vital technical component of knowledge management. The idea is to facilitate the creation of new knowledge by capturing information, identifying patterns, performing analysis, and making the analysis available to other users when they need it. Explicit knowledge that is of high value, or for which substantial resources have been expended to create, always merits some level of management.

Linking documents and content to people in a corporate environment depends on developing a system that includes components for searching, content organization, collaboration, and learning. Ideally, all these components should be accessible across the enterprise and maintainable over the course of time. Obviously, FileNet offers a powerful platform for content organization and searching, but what about collaboration and learning?

FileNet has been marketed as a KM solution in the past, but it is implemented primarily to solve very specific business issues related to imaging, document management, and workflow. Nearly all business functions need to be documented to record and regulate the activity of the organization. Although many documents are now dynamic, do not underestimate the importance of capturing certain documents in very static formats.

Static documents preserve vital histories by making a snapshot of a moment in time. The importance of this activity has been recognized for thousands of years, since marks were first made on clay tablets to record sales and taxes. Today, as the complexity of business increases, the need for context-preserving technologies, like imaging and workflow, is greater than ever.

A document management system can provide powerful tools to support your organization's KM strategies, but this requires a paradigm shift for project managers and technical workers, due to the differences in the form and function of knowledge management tasks versus document management tasks. In this chapter, we define a strategy for bypassing some of the classic problems that face KM implementations by maximizing the utilization of existing resources.

Contrasting Document and Knowledge Management Systems

Most DM systems support core business tasks such as accounts payable processing, and they are chosen based on firm return-on-investment figures. These existing systems are built with the following assumptions:

- The information contained in the systems must be tightly rationed to prevent misuse.
- Speed of document delivery is a top concern, since workers access the system hundreds of times per day in exactly the same way.
- Security must be tight since it contains highly confidential information, such as Social Security numbers and home addresses.
- Data capture hardware and infrastructure requirements and costs can be heavy due to the need for centralized, high volume, data capture centers.
- Typical KM systems work from a completely different perspective, and the difference needs to be addressed right from the beginning of the project.
- The information contained in the systems should be widely advertised to assure maximum usage.
- Flexibility in the ways to search for information is far more important than the speed of document delivery, because the users access the system very infrequently in ways that are vastly different each time.
- Security must be fairly loose, since any additional access hurdles the users have to leap through discourages usage.
- Data capture hardware and infrastructure requirements are low and often zero in KM systems, since documents are typically

created electronically and uploaded by the authors, eliminating the need for scanners and indexers.

Comparing Document and Knowledge Management Systems

Despite the many differences that separate DM systems from KM systems, in most cases both can peacefully coexist on the same platform, because they have similar resource needs. In fact, many of the technology products in the KM field have backgrounds in imaging and document management. Here are some similarities between document management and imaging technologies:

- Both require a high level of scalability, since they are likely to be implemented across the entire enterprise and accessed from a variety of locations.
- Both require extremely flexible application programming interfaces (APIs), because they often are integrated with other key systems and processes.
- They often require a significant investments in hardware, software, and infrastructure.
- Both provide ROI based on both hard and soft dollar savings but are typically implemented on the basis of hard dollar savings alone.
- Both require an architecture that is modular enough to allow a diverse selection of interfaces, business rules, and workflows.
- Both use technology to enable asynchronous information exchange, which means that a great deal of thought and planning needs to go into considering what types of information needs to be exchanged and how they are to be captured and retrieved.

Clearly, DM systems and KM systems have more commonalities than differences. Therefore, it is reasonable to try to consolidate these functions onto a single platform. Building KM solutions on existing platforms frees up resources to address the critical cultural aspects of KM and helps to avoid spending all of your time shopping for an all-encompassing, out-of-the-box solution that does not exist.

In choosing new platform products for KM activities, you may benefit from "coat-tailing" onto the implementation of more traditional business technologies such as messaging, ERP, document management, and imaging. These technologies are usually better funded, better supported, and given much higher priority than KM-associated products like chat, forums, Web crawlers, portals, peer-to-peer, and social networking software. The key is to find out which traditional technologies offer the potential to support your KM activity goals.

For instance, although FileNet was created as an imaging product, over time the company has added numerous optional components to support a wide range of KM activities, such as application integration, portals, business process management, Web content management, managing best practices, and electronic forms. The company switched tactics by deemphasizing knowledge management. It now focuses its marketing on the ability to provide a platform to support complex processes involving widely dispersed groups of workers. The belief is that the customer base is tactically focused due to budget constraints. Users still demand and buy tools to help them get their work done more cost effectively, while supporting stronger feedback loops behind the scenes.

Many competing products, like Documentum, were designed to manage libraries of digitally created documents rather than images of scanned paper documents. This makes them flexible for WCM functions such as managing the development and maintenance of websites and other dynamic objects. However, it limits their ability to effectively manage images, workflows, and other, more static production-level data objects. Documentum even went to the extra step of purchasing technologies for collaboration and syndication of electronic content. For this reason, many organizations choose Documentum systems for less transactional functions that focus on dialog more than throughput and disaster recovery. However, they often find demonstrating sufficient ROI, in hard dollars, extremely challenging for those systems.

One advantage that products like FileNet have is their ability to bridge the gap between information and accessibility. Every day organizational personnel grow more geographically dispersed, and yet they still act as the primary point of customer contact. These globally dispersed knowledge workers cannot possibly rely on business processes based on shuffling paper documents. Although they need access to key information like insights and best practices, do not underestimate the value of more transactional document types such as contracts, invoices, proposals, HR documents, and other enterprise records.

In knowledge management, organizations seek to change their cultures in profound ways. Today, most knowledge workers spend up to half of their day creating, filing, mailing, finding, or managing different types of content. In most cases, knowledge hoarders fill desk drawers, file cabinets, and computer hard drives with mountains of organizational secrets. The toughest KM task is getting users to *believe* in sharing knowledge. To achieve an acceptable ROI, the strategy should be focused on assigning the best resources to the hardest problems. Obviously, that comes down to the culture and processes as much as the technology.

Catalyst Management for Actionable Knowledge

The argument that knowledge is stored in people begs the question, Then why do knowledge management programs almost always require the large implementation of a content management platform? The answer lies in the way humans communicate. Humans are bound to family, friends, and community. Experiences are a part of this binding and these shared experiences affect communication.

Regardless of the subject, sooner or later someone will find a particular point on which to stir a passionate statement, speech, or debate. Political correctness, which often points out issues that are too sensitive to discuss, has in some ways engaged individuals to talk about those very subjects. The ebb and flow of conversation, dialog, and debate is affected by individual beliefs, experiences, and passions. Sometimes, these beliefs are shared, providing common ground for communication. Other times, conflicting beliefs provide obstacles to understanding, causing words to have different meanings and allow miscommunication.

Therefore, when discussing KM and content management, the thought should not be simply to capture, catalog, and distribute information vital to the business but also to capture the very issues and ideas that forced the original discussion. In other words, not just the ideas are important but also the path that brought the individual or team to those ideas. This content about context is often the very catalyst of innovation.

In discussing catalysts and how they affect KM goals, it is important to understand that individuals often work as idea catalysts for others. There is always someone in an organization that rubs people the wrong way. The question is why, and do they serve any use to the organization? The answer may be discovered if individual's communication style and habits are examined. Is the individual opinionated? Does the individual continually try to shoot down others ideas? Can the individual be used as a catalyst to help improve existing proposed ideas, shake out assumptions, or spur new ideas through the group's passion to prove this person wrong? This type of individual can be difficult to work with but truly serve a purpose. They often teach people civil ways to avoid agreeing with something that is wrong, just to keep the peace. Figure 7.1 shows how important catalysts are to growing organizational knowledge through dialog.

Catalysts spur the consideration and debating of ideas until they become good ideas. However, in the end, someone must take charge

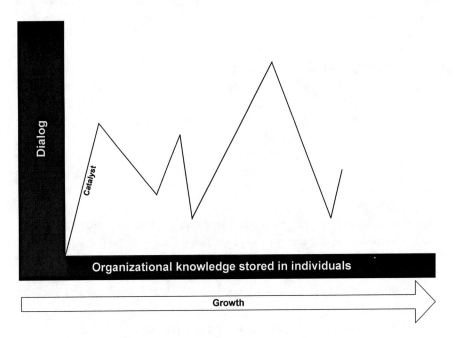

Figure 7.1
Organizational knowledge growth

once the knowledge is deemed actionable. When referring to the way he gained control of the Panama Canal Zone and managed to succeed in the building of the canal, Theodore Roosevelt said, "There was much accusation about my having acted in an 'unconstitutional' manner. I took the isthmus, started the canal, and then left Congress—not to debate the canal, but to debate me. While the debate goes on, the canal does too; and they are welcome to debate me as long as they wish, provided that we can go on with the canal."

Actionable knowledge is knowledge that can be absorbed, applied, and acted on. Some argue that knowledge is merely information if it is not actionable knowledge. Today, actionable knowledge has become vital capital in the conduct of business. Competitive advantage requires greater access to information and, more important, creation of higher levels of actionable knowledge. Success requires valuing the attention of peers without reducing the amount of knowledge sharing.

Four methods are commonly used to reduce vast mountains of unstructured data and information while increasing the attention applied to actionable knowledge that can be absorbed, applied, and acted on:

1. *Pruning.* Eliminate obsolete, irrelevant, inaccurate, and out-of-date information. Removing wood makes the tree stronger.
2. *Capturing context.* Summary, analysis, comparison, synthesis, and conclusions all help increase the amount of actionable knowledge in documents.
3. *Presentation.* Effective illustration, interactivity, creative staging, and inspirational storytelling inspire others to take action.
4. *Selecting the medium.* Consider the full spectrum of media available for delivery of the message; different media offer different advantages. Remember that synchronous media improve attention to the message, and asynchronous media improve retention of the message. Be sure to focus on your actual needs and not simply what the vendor wants to sell. Media include:
   - Internet and intranet sites (asynchronous sharing).
   - Video displays and teleconferencing (synchronous sharing).
   - Slide-based presentations (synchronous sharing).

- Phone calls or face-to-face communication (synchronous sharing).
- Hard-copy reports, e-mail, or faxes (asynchronous sharing).
- Direct mail or courier (asynchronous sharing).

Too often, companies fail to realize the importance of these four activities when they plan their document management systems. This has resulted in a growing desire to convert huge data stores into actionable knowledge, by deploying knowledge discovery and data (KDD) mining applications.

Typically, these technologies work via sophisticated pattern analysis, consideration of prior knowledge, statistical inference, and advanced algorithms that analyze massive amounts of data. These technologies are *not* cheap and early results have been mixed. So far, software simply cannot mimic the judgment of people. When you consider the high price of any enterprise-level KDD application, you have to wonder why most companies still consider employees as expenses and the desks they sit at as assets. Often, the best KDD system available is a strong, ongoing dialog within a large group of diverse people.

SHARED ABSTRACTION MEANS COMMON GROUND

Abstraction is the process of removing characteristics of something to reduce it to a set of essential characteristics. Humans do this instinctively as they examine their surroundings and solve problems. The process of abstraction relies on setting a goal, defining a data representation, identifying relevant features, and categorizing the results. Like a library, the value of an abstraction is as much in what it leaves out as in what it includes.

Computers do not handle abstractions as well as humans, but humans must be trained to use this very natural talent consistently in business. Part of this process is agreeing on a common language by which the community can communicate. The humans who operate your business are individuals that have individual passions, backgrounds, and beliefs. A common language brings individuals together in a way that they can communicate with less frustration brought on by a communication barrier. The idea is to create common ground without sacrificing the diversity of experience, opinion, and thought.

The process of abstraction uses the technique of ignoring a subset of characteristics and features of a subject. This allows other characteristics to be generalized in an attempt to identify the relevant similarities and patterns. Comparing the results of these generalizations often leads to powerful insights and actionable knowledge. A simple example might be the way networking professionals often describe their technologies in plumbing terms. Ideas like pipes, connectors, flow rates, and leakage fit well in describing network issues; and they often point toward potential solutions. Although everything that is true for plumbing is not necessarily true for networking, the abstraction provides a useful catalyst for new ideas.

In the movie *The Gods Must Be Crazy*, a pilot drops a Coca-Cola bottle from his airplane window and deposits a piece of trash deep in the African jungle. A native of a very remote tribe finds the bottle and takes it home. Over the next few weeks, the bottle becomes the center of wonder, experimentation, and discovery for the tribe. Through the native's built-in ability of abstraction, the tribe discovers multiple ways the bottle could be used to improve individuals' lives in the village.

Vigorous debate over the possibilities of the bottle gives way to jealousy and a desire to control this gift from the gods. As the chief observes the issues that begin to arise around the bottle and because he has past experience to draw from, he orders the native who discovered the curse sent by the gods to get rid of it far from the accessibility of the community. Even though the bottle was *not* a curse sent from the gods, the chief found the abstraction useful because it brought the tribe a solution to their problem. If the chief had been instructed on the manufacture of Coke bottles, the lesson would be worthless, as the knowledge would not be actionable nor would it address the tribe's problem.

Regardless of what individuals find before them, they will use their experiences, knowledge, and abstraction to solve its mystery or at the very least build a language to describe it. Most of us accept that we are shaped by our individual experiences, but most of us do not realize that we also are prisoners of our experiences. Despite outward appearances, we *all* experience reality in our own ways. Sometimes, this leads us more quickly to unique insights; other times, it blinds us to obvious opportunities. A diversity of abstractions, shared in constant dialog among the stakeholders, is the best protection from this type of blindness.

FileNet—Improving Attention and Retention

Today, most companies understand the critical nature of e-mail systems to the success of their organization. E-mail enables individuals to communicate asynchronously and have dialog that spans different time zones and work schedules. Before e-mail, time delays in communication greatly affected the effectiveness of the message. Although the telephone is a great technology, it is limited by the individual's availability (synchronous), whereas e-mail will wait to deliver its message (asynchronous). E-mail also has the advantage of being able to carry visual aids to the recipient to better communicate the message's intent.

Similar to how e-mail has added to communication, an enterprise content manager like FileNet can hold the catalysts of innovation until a leader comes along to act on them. Innovation typically arrives in the order of ideas, expertise, and leadership. This is because someone has to be inspired with a dream, then the technical expertise must be developed, and finally someone must step up and lead. Skip any step in this hierarchy of innovation and you reach no actionable knowledge. One thing that make this so difficult to achieve in organizations is that often a member of a different work group must take each step.

For something to be considered useful knowledge, it must be actionable. For ideas to be acted on requires the expertise and a authority to act. It is therefore easy to understand why organizations that have generated great ideas seem to have difficulty acting on them. The added obstacle of every group of people working from somewhat different abstractions makes the confluence of ideas, expertise, and leadership seem as rare and illusive as true love.

Of the Fortune 100 companies, 93 use FileNet systems today. This gives those companies a base of existing equipment, applications, and experience from which to capture ideas and expertise that can be used with leadership to create innovation catalysts. Capturing ideas and expertise is only part of the equation. A good idea or even actionable knowledge leads to innovation only in the presence of both attention and retention by peers. This is where FileNet comes in, not as the vehicle of KM but as the road that enables the vehicle to operate.

Applying Learning to Organizational Processes

An organization must continually be aware of its surrounding environment. Like any animal in nature, organizations face a rapidly changing environment, predators, and social issues. Because organizations that are not alert can be damaged or destroyed, they need to continually use their senses and instincts. Problem recognition usually occurs at the front lines of a business, but many communication channels are too focused on top-down messages to allow problems to escalate upward efficiently.

Animals adapt to environmental changes, such as droughts, by adapting their bodies to operate leaner and conserve water. Organizations too often fail to sense the economic drought coming or fail to prepare plans for such environmental changes. Animals have the advantage of built-in instinct to guide their actions, but organizations have their own advantage, people. Organizations need to continue to learn new ways to harness the intellectual power of the individuals that are a part of their organization.

In the IT world, "grid computing" is quickly gaining popularity as a way to add processing power through linking many processors. In the same way, organizations need quick ways to project the current issues the organization faces to the mass organizational populace for ideas. Naturally, some issues require confidentiality or must be secure because of laws that prevent the sharing that information. This does not remove the authority or responsibility of leadership to make decisions, but it allows for new ideas to flow upward and gives an opportunity for providing feedback.

When organizations are polled, individuals deep within an organization often surprise their peers and leadership by offering exciting innovations that improve the overall process efficiency. These innovations sometimes reflect the removal of labor-intensive steps that do little to help the process or allow technology to combine steps to reduce the wasted attention of the individuals tied to the process.

As you move down the hierarchy of an organization the compensation drops, but the number of members per level increases. Improving processes at the lower levels can return a sizable decrease in costs. Managing and leveraging the organization's intellectual assets can also improve the overall communication among levels, by demonstrating the value an organization places in individual input.

Speeding these types of innovations requires a disciplined planning process that is put into place prior to a need arising. Plans should be made to include short-term and long-term ways to improve operations to increase efficiently. Short-term solutions include activities that improve efficiency or reduce cost but are not sustainable over a long period. Organizations making their lists of these short-term activities should organize them by cost, ease, and speed of implementation. Then, when environmental changes happen, these short-term solutions can be rushed into action.

An organization needs to evaluate long-term solutions in a similar way. Long-term solutions typically have more complexity but often can be implemented before change forces the issue. These strategic evolutions often change the operation of the organization forever and increase its opportunity for survival. Long-term solutions are more likely to address the fundamental problems within a system, but they usually require more research, more analysis, and greater levels of shared vision. One document-based tool for increasing the feeling of shared mission within an organization is the balanced scorecard.

Balancing Departmental Goals with Balanced Scorecards

Balanced scorecards and organizational development have been hot trends for several years, and research has shown that building good, understandable feedback loops can improve both efficiency and morale. However, in many cases, scorecards simply did not work because of the metrics tracked, the way the information was communicated to the organization, or the culture itself.

Even if you decide that a balanced scorecard is not for you, knowing about scorecard tools can be helpful, since some of the tools can be used independently. A balanced scorecard is a consolidated list of numbers that reflect the performance of an organization based on such areas as financials, customers, processes, learning, suppliers, people, and support systems (see Figure 7.2). The metrics should measure not just important outcomes but also the factors that influence those outcomes.

The basic philosophy of the balanced scorecard is that people will focus on what is being measured—more because it shows what is cared about than because of financial incentives. This gives company leaders a strong communication tool for pointing to where attention

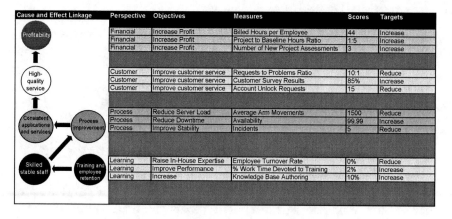

Cause and Effect Linkage	Perspective	Objectives	Measures	Scores	Targets
Profitability	Financial	Increase Profit	Billed Hours per Employee	44	Increase
	Financial	Increase Profit	Project to Baseline Hours Ratio	1.5	Increase
	Financial	Increase Profit	Number of New Project Assessments	3	Increase
High-quality service	Customer	Improve customer service	Requests to Problems Ratio	10:1	Reduce
	Customer	Improve customer service	Customer Survey Results	85%	Increase
	Customer	Improve customer service	Account Unlock Requests	15	Reduce
Consistent applications and services / Process improvement	Process	Reduce Server Load	Average Arm Movements	1500	Reduce
	Process	Reduce Downtime	Availability	99.99	Increase
	Process	Improve Stability	Incidents	5	Reduce
Skilled stable staff / Training and employee retention	Learning	Raise In-House Expertise	Employee Turnover Rate	0%	Reduce
	Learning	Improve Performance	% Work Time Devoted to Training	2%	Increase
	Learning	Increase	Knowledge Base Authoring	10%	Increase

Figure 7.2
Balanced scorecard example

needs to be applied. Within most organizations, an individual's actual behavior often focuses on financial measures, but that may not always help the person improve his or her results. Why? Because if you tell your employees to increase shareholder value, how are they supposed to know what to do?

First, determine what constitutes building shareholder value. Is it high customer loyalty, high quality, or low-priced products? Once that has been determined, the balanced scorecard is used to communicate these measurements regularly. This provides the team with a regularly reoccurring opportunity to improve. Identifying the most critical areas for improvement is often all employees need to start changing their behaviors. Empirical research and a history of success stories show that strategic measurement methods like balanced scorecards can work wonders. However, in many cases, scorecards alone simply do not work. Process flaws are often the culprits.

Process Evolution

An example of an organization improving its processes is given in Figure 7.3, which looks at a typical accounts payable process and some of the evolutions it has gone through. This diagram looks only at the invoice approver's component of the process.

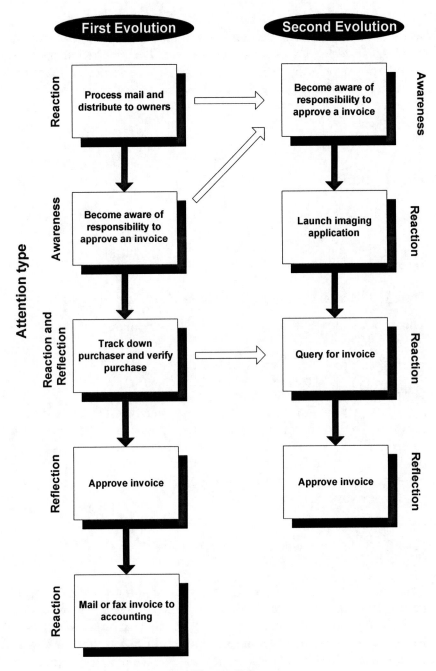

Figure 7.3
Evolving an existing process

Figure 7.3 is split into two main columns, first evolution and second evolution. These columns represent the changes that happen in an organization as the process improves. The diagram also examines the process from the perspective of the three types of attention: awareness, reaction, and reflection. Workers perform their best when all three types of attention are maximized and focused on the business process.

First Evolution

In the first evolution, the process represents a basic paper invoice management process and assumes that an enterprise resource planning system exists within the accounting department.

Step 1. Process Mail and Distribute It to Owners

This process box represents the manual processing of mail at the different field locations. This process is replaced, in the second evolution, by centralized image capture and an ERP e-mail notification of an invoice awaiting approval. The type of attention typically used during this process is reaction.

Typically, reactions are based on previously established procedures. If reactions become a problem area in a process, you may need to reconsider your procedures. Even the "best practices" become obsolete over time, and often the mere act of creating formal documentation for a process points out logical problems and opportunities for improvement.

Step 2. Become Aware of the Responsibility to Approve the Invoice

This process box represents the attention required to recognize the need for action and understand one's responsibilities. The attention used during this process is awareness. In many cases, awareness is limited by poor notification mechanisms and other technologies that do not value attention. Portal technologies often attempt to improve information awareness by reducing the number of user interfaces required for job performance. Other awareness improving technologies include monitoring software, automated escalation systems, subscription systems, and syndication of content.

Step 3. Track down the Purchaser and Verify the Purchase

In a semimanual process, significant legwork can be required to reconcile an invoice to the original purchaser or requester to ensure that the item purchased indeed was received. The attention typically used during this process is both reaction and reflection.

Step 4. Approve the Invoice

During this process step, the individual with approval authorization approves the invoice by reconciling it with receipts and any additional background information and manually approving the invoice. The attention typically used during this process is reflection. Reflection is called for when predefined procedures are not sufficient to resolve an issue. Reflection is a uniquely human activity where users strive for answers based on available information and their own past experiences. Typically, tasks that involve high degrees of reflection, such as exception handling, are extremely difficult to automate.

Step 5. Mail or Fax the Invoice to Accounting

This step of the process typically concludes the approval process and begins the next accounting process of paying the invoice (not shown). The approver or an administrative assistant may handle this step. The attention typically used during this process is reaction. This concludes the first evolution column.

Second Evolution

This column represents the first round of automation made to the approvers' process. In the first evolution, the process was a basic paper process and assumes an enterprise resource planning system exists within the accounting department. The second evolution incorporates the ERP system with an e-mail system and an imaging system to provide a notification to the approver in the field. The notification makes the user aware that he or she has an invoice to view in the imaging system and approve within the ERP system.

To facilitate these changes, all vendors doing business with the organization have to be notified of the address for a new centralized scanning and capture center for the organization. Instead of mailing invoices to one of a number of business locations, the vendors are required to mail the invoices to the new centralized scanning and capture center. Because approvers in the field require viewing the invoice before approving it, an imaging component is added to the approval process.

Step 1. Become Aware of Responsibility to Approve the Invoice

This process box represents the attention required to understand one's responsibilities and possibly learn or review the process and procedures required to complete the activity that comes with this responsibility. During this step, a notification is received by the approver, making him or her aware of an invoice awaiting approval in the ERP system. The time required to become aware of the need to verify an invoice for approval is drastically reduced because users watch their e-mail in-boxes for changes much more closely than they watch the ERP system.

Step 2. Launch the Imaging Application

During this evolution of the process the imaging application is tied to the ERP solution, but both must be launched and logged in to. The attention that is typically used during this process is reaction. A user reacts to the need to verify an invoice by finding and launching the imaging application and querying for the invoice that they need to see. Although training users to find invoices in the imaging system can be somewhat costly and time consuming, it is much quicker and easier than digging through file cabinets and desktops.

Step 3. Query for the Invoice

Both the ERP and the imaging application require user knowledge of the individual interfaces for navigating to the invoice data record and invoice image. The attention typically used during this process is reaction. The user reacts to the invoice verification notice by both launching the imaging application and following the query procedures previously set up. The problems come in when procedures become inconsistent or are simply not defined at all.

Step 4. Approve the Invoice

During this process step the individual with approval authorization approves the invoice via the ERP application and records any extra comments. The type of attention used during this process is reflection, and this is the key activity of this particular business function.

The main effect in automating the approval process is a reduction in the time required by the approver to handle the paperwork. Additional benefits include keeping the invoice and all relevant information pertaining to the invoice available as well as removing the need for packaging and mailing the invoice information to the Accounting Department.

One drawback of this evolution is that it does not remove complexity for the approver: The approver has fewer steps but must be trained to understand the ERP system and the imaging system. Also, more time is spent reacting than reflecting.

As the process continues to evolve, we see additional improvements through the refining of systems and procedures. Figure 7.4 compares the second evolution with the third evolution.

Third Evolution

The right column, third evolution, represents the second round of automation made to the approvers' process. In the second evolution, the process incorporated the ERP system with the e-mail system to provide the approver in the field notification that he or she has an invoice to approve within the ERP system. The third evolution picks up at this point and pushes forward.

The third evolution integrates the ERP system, imaging system, and e-mail system to a Web application that maintains a client relationship with the ERP system. Nightly extracts keep the Web application up-to-date and preclude the need for the approver to log into the ERP system. The Web system is also linked to the imaging application and maintains a direct link to the images via URLs.

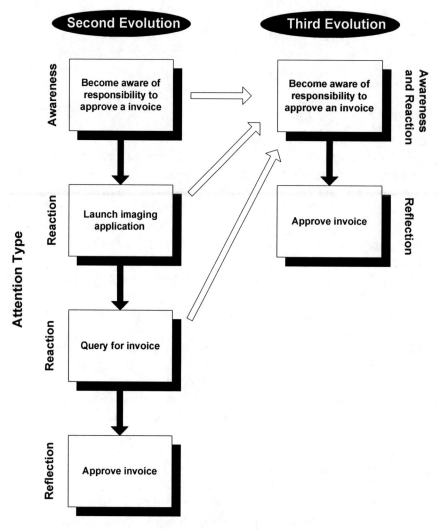

Figure 7.4
Continuing process evolution, the third evolution

The result is a much more user-friendly system, with automated workflow to assure consistent procedures. Other benefits from this evolution include the ability to reduce user software licensing costs and eliminate the need for training invoice approvers on how to query the imaging system.

Step 1. Become Aware of the Responsibility to Approve the Invoice

During this process step, the approver in the field receives an e-mail that he or she has an invoice that needs approval. The e-mail contains a URL link to the image that requires no navigational training to understand. The e-mail also contains the ERP record's information embedded in the e-mail, removing the need for the approver to log into the ERP system. Although the approver is still required to know his or her responsibility for approving organizational invoices, the amount of time and attention that this process requires has been greatly reduced.

Step 2. Approve the Invoice

During this final process step, the individual with approval authorization approves the invoice by choosing a link embedded in the notification e-mail. The embedded link functionality sends an update to the ERP system for posting. The type of attention typically used during this process is reflection.

The impact in this evolution is the reduced approval process steps facilitated through the automation of the e-mail notification and the strict management of workflow. These improvements reduce the time required by the approver to handle the entire process and allows for critical attention to be focused on the individual's primary job function. The new process is focused more on reflection, because many of the reactions have been automated and awareness has been reduced.

One drawback of the second evolution is that it does not remove complexity. The approver has fewer steps than before but requires training to understand the ERP system and the imaging system. The third evolution reduces complexity and any retraining could probably be handled via a document e-mailed to the approvers.

These examples have been high level, and it is easy for the reader to ask why not just jump to the third evolution from the beginning? Although that conclusion may be easy to draw from the provided information, real world situations are much more complex and seldom well documented. Individuals in the field using these processes everyday are full of excellent ideas for improvements. Their suggestions may need refining and technical input, but bringing them together with technically savvy analysts pays off. Workflow management systems make creating these feedback loops much easier.

Using Workflows to Add Structure to Data

The FileNet Corporation produces a vast array of products focused mostly on managing unstructured data and managing workflows. Unstructured data represent one of the most vulnerable areas of most organizations today, and workflows are one of the strongest ways to gain control over unstructured data.

Managing unstructured data is like herding cattle, it is slow, dirty work. Organizing unstructured data can be terribly cumbersome. FileNet's management tools allow organizations to take this information and harness it into powerful workflows that provide for more automation, accountability, and more dynamic feedback loops.

In Figure 7.5, unstructured data lie as a roadblock in the business flow. The reason it is a roadblock in most organizations is their inability to gain actionable information from the data. This typically results in labor-intensive work-arounds that are unable to capture the true value of the unstructured data.

When the business flow hits the unstructured data, it splits into two streams, one fork flows into a procedural work-around able to

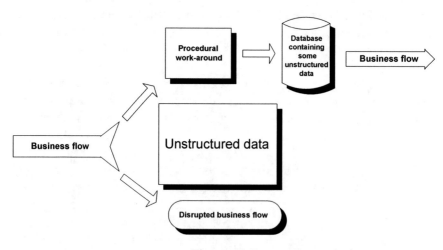

Figure 7.5
Roadblock caused by unstructured data

capture some of the unstructured data to use as the business flow resumes. The second fork represents the lost initiative and business flow that to often happens when organizations fail in their attempt to use unstructured data.

To harness unstructured data, a context needs to be captured (preferably at receipt or creation) and added into an object manager that serves the organization's business need. FileNet's object managers include imaging, workflow, document management, and Web content services. Imaging, content, and document management all enable the manipulation of unstructured data, but the workflow components best exploit the unstructured data. In Figure 7.6, the workflow manages the unstructured data using FileNet tools and resumes the business flow carrying the relevant unstructured data along in a database feed.

This is a very high-level view but only to make an important point about the crippling impact of unstructured data. Every organization has some unstructured data, how it chooses to deal with the data drives its adaptability and survivability.

FileNet tools, like many other toolsets, can be used to overcome the issues described in the unstructured data diagrams; however, business expertise is needed to make the workflows a reality. FileNet can provide the document management experience needed or an organization can employ a FileNet ValueNet partner. In either case, the FileNet expert's knowledge must align with the business expert's knowledge. Their competing objectives must be balanced and expectations set accurately.

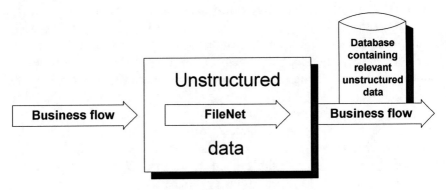

Figure 7.6
Dealing with unstructured data

Some organizations may be uninterested in a FileNet ValueNet partnership and have reasons for not wanting to purchase resources directly from FileNet. In these situations, the organization should look to the large consulting firms like IBM. In addition to IBM's own imaging offering, it also manages some very large FileNet installations and has developed strong centers of expertise. The tools and expertise are available, so organizations no longer have excuses for not attacking the unstructured data issue.

Success Story

A county's assistance department is faced with new state and federal government regulations requiring the collection of documentation from applicants and recipients of human services. The federal agency hopes to inform decision makers with well-analyzed aggregate information. Unfortunately, the department's ability to comply is limited because case folders containing critical documents are kept by individual caseworkers.

Because of a previous success using FileNet, the county again turns to FileNet to help develop a solution. Using FileNet's capture professional and image services products, the county begins capturing all the incoming content electronically, including forms, personnel documents, applications, and faxes. Once captured, the documents are distributed to caseworkers via online in baskets and stored centrally in electronic folders, where all the content is organized by document type, case number, and client name.

The solution enabled the county to save 35,000 hours per year through ease of access and the use of online forms and fax capabilities. Additional improvements include the ability to access content quickly, easily, and simultaneously by multiple workers. Even while undergoing staff reductions, customer service was improved, storage of paper documents was reduced, and 3000 square feet of valuable office space was reclaimed. In addition to meeting the federal guidelines, the new system delivered improved customer service by enabling the workers to respond faster to service and information requests, and it eliminated the need for clients to resubmit information when seeking additional services or benefits.

Chapter 8

FILENET AND ENTERPRISE RESOURCE PLANNING

One machine can do the work of 50 ordinary men. No machine can do the work of one extraordinary man.

—Elbert Hubbard (1856–1915)

KEY OBJECTIVES

- Understand that ERP applications are used to carry out common business functions usually based on very document-centric processes.
- Recognize the need for ERP systems to be integrated with other strategic computing resources, such as imaging applications, mainframe applications, and sales databases.
- Understand how to implement ERP integration solutions that are secure and flexible enough to extend outside the organizational boundaries.

141

- Become familiar with ServerLink (formerly known as ArchiveLink), the approved application program interface for connecting document management systems to SAP.
- Learn the different types of archiving relevant within an SAP system and understand the differences between late, early, and simultaneous archiving.
- Understand the capabilities of the FileNet middleware component Document Warehouse for SAP™.

Enterprise Resource Planning

An important topic when discussing imaging solutions is enterprise resource planning integration. Since the level of integration varies by product and project design, it pays to research this issue thoroughly before any ERP implementation. Another key factor in the ERP arena is whether the design, oversight, and implementation should be handled internally or externally.

ERP applications are used to carry out common business functions, such as financial management, plant maintenance, order entry, procurement, billing, warehousing, transportation, and human resource. Centralizing these key functions in a database application allows executives a bird's-eye view of their operations to observe major trends and still enabling them "drilling down" to troubleshoot a single transaction.

The importance of these applications often requires organizational IT departments to integrate their ERP systems with other strategic computing resources, such as imaging applications, mainframe applications, and sales databases. Most ERP solutions have basic imaging functionality built-in, along with APIs to integrate other imaging systems, applications, and workflows. The major ERP vendors include SAP, PeopleSoft, Oracle, and Baan.

Typically, ERP solutions are at the very heart of organizational initiatives to automate business processes. Often these initiatives require the reengineering of internal processes to match the design of the ERP solution being implemented. Most ERP-savvy consulting organizations tell you that altering the default ERP processes creates significant risk during system upgrades. This calls for significant planning to create integration points that are effective and sustainable.

SAP does not provide enterprise content management capabilities. However, to perform business tasks efficiently, SAP users need easy access to an external content management system containing related, unstructured information. Document Warehouse for SAP (DWSAP) document linking and viewing enables SAP users to easily find, manage, and link externally stored documents to SAP transactions and enables faster processing of payments and other activities.

Another complexity to imaging integration with ERP solutions is that the ERP solution may extend outside the organization's boundaries and require the imaging solution to be flexible and secure enough to handle this. If the goal is supply line integration, you can expect to have to open part of your network to outside users, such as vendors, customers, and new clients. This type of openness can create some complex networking issues, but the payoff is often massive. The DWSAP software integrates the FileNet and SAP applications via the SAP ServerLink interface. *Warning*: This application was formerly known as and is still often referred to as *ArchiveLink*. See Figure 8.1 for an overview of a common FileNet/SAP integration scenario.

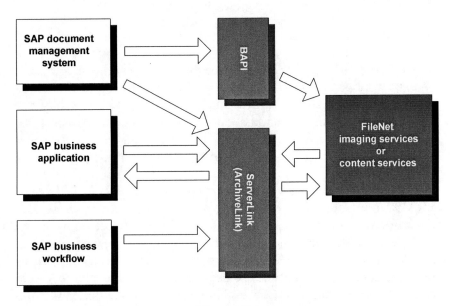

Figure 8.1
SAP and FileNet communication

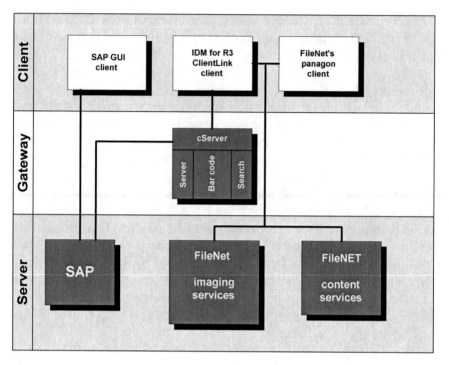

Figure 8.2
Integration layers

It is helpful to understand the three main layers of the imaging and content management integration to any ERP solution. The three integration layers are client, gateway, and server (see Figure 8.2). Each layer contains components that affect other components in other layers. SAP is used in the following list to demonstrate these zones and the FileNet products that support each zone of integration.

- *Gateway integration.* The starting point for platform-to-platform integration is a common set of protocols that allows different systems to communicate with each other. Encapsulating integration components into the portals or gateways between systems can make connecting them together as simple as scripting tasks within a graphical user interface. Gateway integration allows advanced functions such as bar code indexing and automatic document or data capture from fax- and Web-based electronic forms.

■ *Server integration.* In mixed computing environments, essential data may be held in an unwieldy combination of proprietary database and storage servers. Standards such as XML and technologies including data transformation services give users the ability to access and query the information they need without having to worry about where it resides or how it is stored.

■ *Client integration.* As the power of an existing infrastructure expands by adding new functions and services, it is critical that the new technologies operate well with existing applications, business rules, and data formats. Integrating multiple systems within a single interface can be beneficial in improving process speed and reducing training costs. Minimizing the number of custom interfaces an employee must learn can also reduce help desk calls. Integrating your processes to include fewer interfaces helps make sure the solution to data overload does not become part of the problem.

These complexities often lead major companies to seek out imaging and document management systems "certified" by their ERP vendor. Becoming certified requires creating an integration point through an API approved by the ERP vendor. For example, a Business API or BAPI is an interface to one of SAP's R/3 applications. It enables third-party developers to write enhancements that interact with the R/3 modules. Once the middleware has been written, it is submitted for review and testing by the ERP vendor. If cleared, the ERP provider certifies the middleware product and makes a commitment not to break the integration point during regular upgrade cycles.

This keeps middleware software developers from wasting their time, customers from wasting their money, and allows the ERP vendor to manage strategic alliances with other software makers. The approved API for connecting document management systems to SAP is called *ServerLink* (formerly *ArchiveLink*) *for R/3*, FileNet created the middleware component Document Warehouse for SAP to meet this specification.

Document Warehouse for SAP

Document Warehouse for SAP enables SAP's business applications to access FileNet document images, as well as providing document and data archiving for SAP. The application consists of two key components: IDM Services for R/3 and IDM Desktop for R/3. IDM Services for R/3 provides server-side integration and IDM Desktop for R/3 provides client-side integration for use on a desktop or Web server.

SAP ServerLink connects SAP systems to document management systems that utilize SAP's API to build a connection. Most major imaging and document management software companies have written components for ServerLink. SAP integrates with the various imaging and document management systems via a standard set of messages that perform the following ServerLink functions:

- Process incoming documents before, during, or after SAP archiving.
- Link incoming documents to SAP transactions.
- Link incoming documents to workflow items being processed in SAP.
- Archive ongoing documents generated in SAP into the FileNet system.
- Retrieve and display documents linked to SAP transactions.
- Automatically store data archiving files and provide access as needed.

In the SAP world, an *archive* is defined as a logical representation of a physical storage system. With the DWSAP 5.0 release, customers can work with both major interface methods: thick client and Web. Both IDM Desktop and the thin-client Web viewer can be used with SAP via the ServerLink middleware integration component.

Client Integration

FileNet Image Services offers many different ways to integrate clients with ERP solutions and other software packages. With the major ERP solutions FileNet offers tight client integration. The client integration is referred to as *tight* when the ERP solution maintains the overall control, passing the user to the imaging application when necessary and then returning the users back to a refreshed ERP interface on exiting the image viewer (see Figure 8.3).

With "tight" integration, the end user is often unaware that he or she has launched an application outside of the ERP solution. The

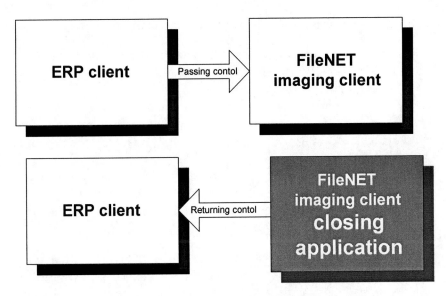

Figure 8.3
Tight integration between FileNet and SAP

ERP application launches the imaging application and passes the critical object information to the imaging application that, depending on how the application is configured, may or may not require a second login.

Without "tight" client integration, the user is required to launch the imaging application and manually transfer the key index field data to the imaging application search interface. This follows the customary login security verification stage. Such "loose" integration has some benefits, including making it somewhat easier to troubleshoot application failures, but most users prefer the speed and ease of use offered by tight integration.

ARCHIVING WITH FILENET

When implementing business application software, application data archiving should be taken into account right from the outset. Since volumes of transaction and master data can expand rapidly in the course of productive operations, consider how to ease the pressure on the database.

Some side effects of rapid SAP system growth are these:

- Since the physical tables are usually stored on hard disks directly attached to the database server, an increase in storage requirements is unavoidable.
- Due to an increase in administration, in an effort to support the database, maintenance windows (system backup, table maintenance, and so forth) claim increasingly unacceptable amounts of time.
- The increased number of rows per database table delays basic operations (searching tables, print jobs, and so forth). The accumulation of these delays leads to a degradation of response times when accessing the data.

ERP solutions generate vast quantities of data, which often must be maintained for years; for this reason, FileNet with its design for long-term storage is an excellent choice for ERP archival storage. SAP recommends archiving application data to reduce database growth and improve system performance; this means moving SAP data from SAP database tables to a FileNet system. Archiving frees up the ERP database and optimizes the system's performance.

According to FileNet, only about 15% of SAP installations have implemented a third-party archiving solution.

Companies typically implement FileNet's DWSAP product to enable the following features and functionality:

- Save training costs by providing easy access to image or document content, stored in a FileNet system, via folders or queues from within SAP.
- Archive SAP data for later use by utilizing the SAP ServerLink and DMS (SAP's Document Management System) standard APIs for linking FileNet content to SAP records or documents.
- Sharing documents like POs, invoices, vouchers statements, remittances, correspondence, material safety sheets, certificates, drawings, proofs of delivery, and reports.

Every business process uses documents, and most of those documents are still in paper form. However, the continued development of business-to-business (B2B) data exchange demands instantaneous, global access to documents and the information stored in them. Any company or department that supports B2B efforts can gather substantial savings through the electronic archiving of documents. These benefits can include faster processing, reduced costs, shortened response times, and better ways to meet legal requirements for storing data.

Types of Archiving within SAP

The three basic classes of archiving are inbound archiving, outbound archiving, and data archiving.

Inbound Document Archiving

Inbound document archiving links inbound documents, captured into image services or content services, to an SAP record. Most ERP-related imaging needs relate to inbound document archiving, of which there are three primary types:

1. *Early archiving.* Support staff scan documents when they arrive at the company, often performing indexing later in the process. To gain the maximum advantage from this approach, some organizational and process issues must be addressed. The benefits can be significant and usually much greater than in the late archiving approach, since it is so easy to use early archiving with manual or automated workflow systems to globalize business processes. In connection with early archiving, many companies use late archiving to handle exceptions.
2. *Late archiving.* Dedicated data capture staff scan documents after paper versions are processed. Once the documents are processed (e.g., a purchase invoice is entered, checked, authorized, and posted), employees then batch-scan and -process the documents, so they are accessible via the ERP system. A very common way of enabling this is to apply a bar code sticker to the front of each document during document sorting. The bar code number is then captured into the ERP database, which facilitates the storage of a link between the scanned image and the related ERP data *without* requiring significant changes to the business process or manual data entry.
3. *Simultaneous archiving.* It is possible to extract information automatically from the imaged documents via OCR. Software

tools are available that "learn" to recognize certain types of scanned images (e.g., is the image an invoice and, if so, from which supplier or is it correspondence, statement, or the like) and process them according to previously established business rules. This delivers the benefit of removing the need to have indexers key in data, however it usually requires some ongoing quality control. It usually works best in low-volume environments with extremely consistent documents coming in.

Outbound Document Archiving

Capturing outbound documents can be used to improve workflow, accountability, and processing efficiency. Outgoing documents include quotations, sales invoices, delivery notes, certificates, purchase orders, and the like. Furthermore, long-term access to periodically created reports is often required. Additionally, some systems produce lists of documents, containing links to original documents.

Implementing a document management solution for outbound documents can dramatically reduce photocopying, printing, and postage costs. To be prepared for regulatory auditing, many types of documents have to be archived in a way that allows them to be easily retrieved to electronic formats via bulk queries.

Data Archiving

When implementing business application software, application data archiving has to be taken into account right from the outset. Many ERP systems experience volume-related problems as early as 15–18 months after going into production, depending on the modules implemented and the number of transactions processed. Often the choice is made to simply throw more disk and CPU resources at the problem; but it frequently requires upgrading the development, question and answer, and production machines in parallel. Also more and more database administrators may need to be employed, increasing the time it takes to back up the system.

The best solution is to archive the data to some external media, physically deleting data from the database as it is archived. This keeps the database at a constant, predictable size; reduces growth of the disk farm; maintains performance; and over time can lead to a two-thirds reduction in total cost of ownership. Optical media, although slower than magnetic, usually satisfies the most stringent legal requirements; and the data still are centrally accessible, although not directly online.

Results and achievements are noticeable after the data archiving project has been completed in the production system. Changes in system performance and in backup and administration time are especially apparent, although it is difficult to measure improvements in these areas prior to the project. Hardware cost assessments, however, can be estimated using the current database growth, along with the cost of additional hardware resources needed without archiving.

Whatever data archiving option you choose, it should be developed in coordination with any ongoing enterprise data quality management initiatives. A data quality management project has three main segments: data cleanup, data archiving, and data prevention. Each segment can be done separately or in conjunction with the others.

Three Segments of Data Quality Management

1. *Data cleanup*. Data eligible for archiving, due to age, may not be of the necessary status and therefore cannot be archived. This occurs if the business process was not properly closed in SAP, even though the process may be complete from a business point of view. To ensure that all data beyond the specified residence time can be archived, these processes must first be "cleaned up" (completed) in SAP.
2. *Data prevention*. The creation of certain types of data can be deactivated. If you no longer require the data from a business point of view, automatic updating should be deactivated to prevent such data from entering the SAP database. Other types of data can be created on a summarized (aggregated) level, reducing the overall amount of data created.
3. *Data archiving*. This process relocates aging application data attached to completed business transactions and, therefore, no longer needed for online operations. Data are moved from the R/3 database to archive files. Data archiving handles data that cannot be prevented, easily deleted, or that needs to be saved for legal or auditing reasons. FileNet provides an excellent repository for SAP data archiving.

Success Story

The disbursements accounts payable group for an airline is consistently missing tax audit deadlines. In time, the company begins to incur severe penalties. Invoice tracking had become a time-consuming, labor-intensive process that caused delays due to misplaced invoices, which led to angry vendors and missed tax audit deadlines. Eventually, the airline realizes that SAP alone provides insufficient invoice tracking capabilities to meet the company's complex needs.

The airline cannot afford the unplanned expense of these fines and penalties or the overtime costs associated with the paper management tasks of dealing with lost documents. To remedy the situation, the company seeks an automated invoice handling system that would work with SAP and still integrate with an existing purchasing system. This would help improve service to everyone who needs fast, accurate access to invoice data, including vendors, tax auditors, and internal employees.

In the past, approved invoices were received and gathered into folders. Each "keyer" collected a folder of paper invoices, typed them into SAP, then filed each individually into file cabinets. If there was a problem with an invoice, the keyer had to walk the invoice to the appropriate person to solve the problem. In addition to the extra time expended on handling the invoice, this manual process also carried the risk of lost or misplaced paperwork. This inefficient system had a drastic impact on the productivity of everyone processing the invoices.

The airline chooses to leverage an existing relationship with FileNet to implement a new, imaging system within the SAP environment for the accounts payable group. A FileNet Document Warehouse for SAP solution is implemented, using an internal centralized capture department to digitize the incoming invoices on receipt.

With the new FileNet system in place, both SAP users and non-SAP users receive instant access to all invoices in the system. This sent productivity soaring. The time-consuming process of physically routing papers from desk to desk is eliminated, as is the risk of losing or misfiling invoices. Most important, the group began meeting its tax audit deadlines and avoiding fines and penalties.

This solution uses the following four-step data capture process:

1. *Scanning.* Invoices are received by mail and fax. They are prepped for scanning, batched with headers, then scanned and imprinted with an SAP link number. Faxed invoices are received by a FileNet capture application and placed into batches for indexing.
2. *Indexing.* All batched invoices are saved in the FileNet repository and routed through the system to the indexers, who enter index values and route them to distributing.
3. *Distributing.* Based on the index values, the distributors route the invoices to one of several queues, depending on the type and status of the invoice.
4. *Linking.* In an automated linking process, processors enter the SAP link number and invoice number into their automated purchasing and inventory control system. The purchasing and inventory control system processes batch runs nightly and creates SAP invoice transactions.

The benefits of the process improvement include the following:

- Reduced costs associated from manual paper handling labor.
- Elimination of fines due to lost invoice documents and failed tax audits.
- Cost savings from ending the storage of paper invoices with an archive vendor.
- Easier access to invoices by non-SAP users, saving on software licensing costs.
- Improved visibility and tracking of invoices.
- Decreased turn-around time and follow-up on "problem" invoices, through automated exception handling workflow.

Chapter 9

FUNDING AND FILENET

For which of you, intending to build a tower, sitteth not down, first, and counteth the cost, whether he have sufficient to finish, it?

Lest haply, after he hath laid the foundation, and is not able to finish it, all that behold it begin to mock him, saying, this man began to build, and was not able to finish.

—Luke 14:28–30

KEY OBJECTIVES

- Learn tips for preparing to bid and gain approval for a FileNet implementation.
- Become familiar with a number of different FileNet architectural solutions for common content management needs, such as Web interfaces and distributed document capture.
- Learn more about the basic FileNet system architecture and how it manages its memory caches to improve performance.
- Get a general overview of the range of FileNet system licensing costs and what can be expected.
- Understand how to expand the FileNet environment to include a load-balanced Web farm and external production printing and fax servers.

154

- Recognize where to find promising document management supporters within your organization and how to successfully gain funding approval.
- Know how to improve your chances of gaining project-funding approval by combining imaging initiatives with existing knowledge management initiatives within your organization.
- Know the basic job roles and functional issues of data capture center operations.
- Gain a detailed understanding of what resources are required to manage a document imaging project and conversion on a continuous basis.
- Understand how new regulations, such as the Sarbanes-Oxley Act of 2002, create increased need for content management and workflow systems within organizations.

Projecting the Cost

Before an organization leaps into any purchase or project, it must be able to assess the full cost. History is full of stories where the cost was not fully considered, resulting in a failure of some sort. Missing or hidden costs, scope creep, inexperience, and poor project management can affect the cost of a project. These issues must be factored in as possibilities when building an assessment, but first you must capture the big items. This chapter will arm you with information to prepare for bidding and gaining approval for a FileNet implementation.

FileNet purchases are not for the weak of heart or companies that do not plan to be around for long. The dot.com phase of the information age will be remembered for its flashy companies, which made lots of promises and delivered little. These are not the kind of companies that can afford to purchase FileNet or other high-end imaging products. Established companies that seek to build an architecture to support a sustainable future usually put FileNet systems into place. FileNet systems are built to keep information available for decades.

First, an example of a typical FileNet implementation's costs are examined. Second, complexity is added into the model by adding in a distributed capture operation; and finally, we look at a Web-access model with its high-level costs. This is not the final word on FileNet system costs but simply a starting point to begin negotiations and help set expectations.

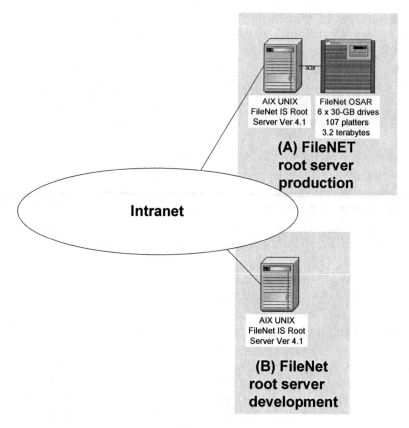

Figure 9.1
*Basic FileNet image services installation: (A) image services and
optical storage, (B) image services development system*

Figure 9.1 shows a basic FileNet image services installation with
no frills at all. The system consists of a primary FileNet Image Services server with attached optical storage unit for generating tranlogs
for disaster backup and a development system that contains everything but the OSAR.

Basic System (AP Configuration)

The installation uses the optical storage and retrieval unit as its
primary storage and a large Page cache to enable quick retrieval of

the most active documents. This type of configuration is good for accounts payables systems because it allows 6–9 months worth of invoices to remain in the Page cache, while the older documents are retrieved from the OSAR when needed. Retrieval time from cache should be 3–5 seconds for a 1–3 page invoice. From the OSAR, it should take between 8–11 seconds, depending on network traffic and configuration.

When evaluating the size of Page cache to determine the disk space needed, compute the total number of monthly invoice pages (*not* documents), times the number of months they need to be available for immediate review, times 50 KB (50,000 bytes). Double this number—that should provide sufficient storage space for the permanent database, Oracle database, BES cache, and Page cache. However, note that most companies plan to roll out a single FileNet system to serve many document types, so build it to scale upward over time.

Figure 9.2 shows the relationship between the two memory caching components of a FileNet application server. Although the BES cache and Page cache are separate, they are tied together when setting up and distributing the overall disk space. It is important to make overall disk space requirements estimates that allow for all four areas together. Later on, allocate the overall cache space as BES cache, Page cache, permanent database, and Oracle database.

Basic System (AP Configuration) FileNet Costs

The system shown in Figure 9.1 is a basic FileNet system built on an accounts payable model, with both the production and development system shown. Table 9.1 contains the FileNet components and their approximate costs. This is a high-level look at typical FileNet system licensing costs and contains none of the labor, hosting, or hardware costs.

Table 9.1 lays out the high-level FileNet costs for the basic system described in Figure 9.1. It does not contain user licenses costs, but it does contain a cost range for an OSAR unit. The unit listed is an OSAR 107HTL, with four 30-GB drives. This unit has 107 optical slots for 30-GB optical platters. The storage capacity for this unit, fully populated with optical platters, is approximately 3.2 terabytes.

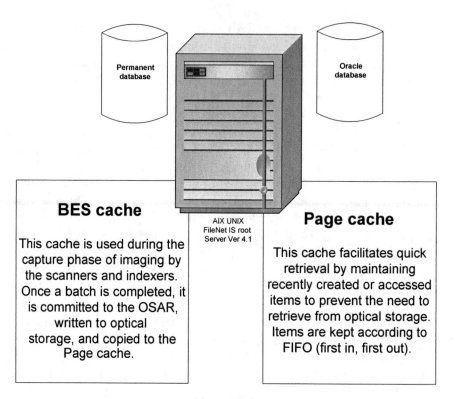

Figure 9.2
FileNet memory cache division

Table 9.1
Typical FileNet Licensing Costs

FileNet Product	Cost Range ($)	
Enterprise image services	38,000	42,000
Optical drivers, high capacity	11,000	13,000
OSAR 107HTL, 4 × 30-GB drives	210,000	260,000
Enterprise image services development	6,000	7,000
Total	265,000	322,000

The Plasmon optical platters used in this OSAR setup are 12" plat-ters, each containing 30 GB of space, and have a cost range of $560–600 each. The approximate media cost for a fully populated OSAR is $59,360–63,600. *Note*: These costs do not include client licenses costs.

Basic System (AP Configuration) with Peripheral Components

In Figure 9.3, we add the peripheral components into the picture. These include fax and print servers and a Web environment.

A Web farm can be very important when considering a FileNet solu-tion. It allows for additional stability for the end users and reduces the overall cost of packaging thick client applications and software pushes to the end users. We cannot overemphasize the importance of good planning when considering a rollout to a large user population.

The figure shows a configuration of a Web farm with four Web servers controlled by a Cisco director (load balancer). The licenses costs for four FileNet Web servers (Web services) are in the range of $4000–6000 each.

The figure also shows the peripheral print and fax environment. The license cost for these products are in the range of $4000–6000 each.

The figure shows a basic FileNet system with addition peripheral environments (Web access and print and fax). The FileNet root servers for production and development are shown as AIX UNIX servers; however, on small systems, these can be NT-based operating systems. (Keep in mind that if an NT-based operating system is used instead of AIX, the auditing capabilities of "check sum" are for-feited.) If the organization plans on more than 70–80 concurrent users, UNIX would be the recommend platform.

The Web environment and the print and fax environments operate on Microsoft NT-based servers. The size of the Web farm is tied directly to the number of concurrent users. A good rule of thumb is approximately 75–80 concurrent users per Web server. If the Web environment includes any customization, a duplicate DEV Web envi-ronment is recommended.

Please note that this Web farm is shown as an intranet-only Web farm. FileNet's products are built to handle the security requirements of the Internet, but it is advisable to build the proper physical network components into the figure to ensure that FileNet security

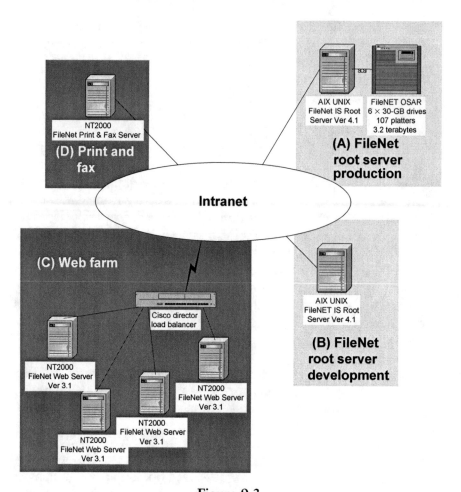

Figure 9.3

*Typical FileNet system including peripheral components: (A)
FileNet image services and optical storage, (B) FileNet image
services development system, (C) Web farm, (D) print and fax*

would be the last line of defense and just a small part of a more
sophisticated overall security plan.

FileNet Clients

Figure 9.4 adds another piece, the Panagon suite. This is the suite of
FileNet client products marketed under the FileNet Panagon name.

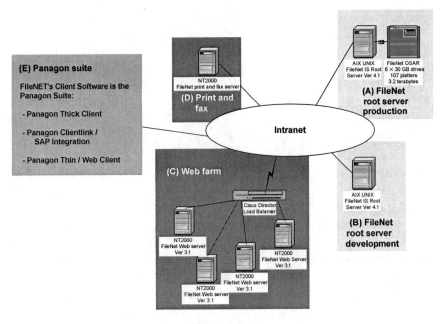

Figure 9.4

Typical FileNet system including client software components:
(A) FileNet image services and optical storage,
(B) FileNet image services development system, (C) Web farm,
(D) print and fax, (E) Panagon suite

User licenses costs vary greatly, depending on the quantity purchased and the savvy of the contract negotiator. For base image services, shared user licenses not including any extras like ERP integration, the cost range is in the ballpark of $3000–5500 per user.

FUNDING STRATEGIES

Funding an expense initiative can be challenging, but projects that include imaging, workflow, and a sound business plan can almost always show significant savings. Process improvements lower overall costs and payoff year after year; therefore, the challenge in getting funding approval for a FileNet implementation initiative is finding the best workflow improvement opportunity and making it a high priority. The key to long-term success is making sure that those process savings exceed the costs of the FileNet system being put into place. This often requires pushing out the usage of this enterprise system to a large group of departments and individuals, to spread out the costs.

A good combination for savings can usually be found in any area of an organization that combines managing large amounts of paper documents with customer service. One of the biggest issues is that few people understand the cost of existing paper systems. Customers never want to wait for an answer and paper document retrieval is inherently slow, error prone, and inefficient. Call centers can offer excellent opportunities to combine applications and improve workflow with good document management.

Another item that makes call centers and customer support centers good candidates for imaging projects is that they already track metrics for response times and the average required time to close a ticket. Reducing document retrieval time in a call center environment always produces significant performance increases. Individuals operating call centers are usually quite willing to become project participants, because they are continually rewarded for improving the efficiency of their centers.

Building the Business Case

In building the business case, project managers must first capture the entire cost of the project, including both implementation and ongoing operations costs. After determining these numbers, the organization should completely map the process that is the focus of improvement. Areas of improvement must be documented and quantified to determine the amount of time and attention that can be removed from the process due to the project implementation. Next, time and attention have to be converted into dollars and cents and compared with the implementation and operations cost model. Finally, the project team must determine whether the dollars add up to justifiable savings.

Sometimes, after completing an assessment that clearly shows strong savings from implementing a project, the pursuit for funding still fails to gain final approval. Often, this is because the business decision makers do not understand the consequences of doing "nothing" on the project. Therefore, doing nothing appears a safer decision.

To reduce the chance of this happening, it is important that the project manager compute the cost of the existing paper-based workflow system. This should be done before the initial proposal is made; because once a proposal has been turned down, it is very difficult to convince leaders that they may have been wrong. Determine the cost annually for using paper, present this first, second show the cost of using an imaging solution, and third compute the saving for the audience.

The strongest cases for imaging projects are typically made around return on investment; however, risk to the organization may soon surpass ROI for the chief reason that organizations implement imaging and workflow. The Sarbanes-Oxley Act of 2002 threatens to turn the business world upside down. To comply, businesses must rethink every process and make those processes clear and concise. Looking into the future, the argument could be made that most organizations will be unable to comply with the Sarbanes-Oxley Act of 2002 without some type of imaging and workflow system.

Combining Initiatives to Gain Project Approval

Because of the cost of high-end imaging systems, it makes sense to combine initiatives whenever possible. One option already mentioned is the idea of joining the imaging initiative with the knowledge management push happening in the organization. Knowledge management is also an initiative that happens in organizations planning for a future and focused on long-term sustainability.

For this marriage to work, however, the environment must believe in the possibilities of all the organization's employees. In a "star culture," the organization has a difficult time justifying combining an imaging initiative to a knowledge management initiative, because a star culture generates too little content. This is because star cultures typically filter out the input of the employees to capture only what some "knowledge auditor" believes relevant.

The Roman empire had a similar star culture of elitism. Because of this culture, the documented working principle of the steam engine was tabled for another millennium and a half after its creation. Imagine how the steam engine, which ushered in the Industrial Age, would have changed history had the Romans not only captured the idea but valued it enough to make it available to others. History has shown how difficult it is to accurately prejudge what information will be valuable in the future.

To prevent a star culture, organizations like IBM build KM communities and implement knowledge-sharing events that deliver the opportunity to share ideas within the organization without the strict filtering. The hoarding and wasting of knowledge and information can be overcome with the right organizational culture.

Like KM, enterprise content management should also be considered when looking for combining initiatives. Both can share infrastructure resources, and separation of the two often leads to the following deficiencies:

- Lack of integration of electronic forms, telephone systems, messaging-based applications, and intranet databases into overall imaging and content management approach—the basics of information management are very similar despite the differing data formats.
- The need to evolve office systems from paper-based to an integrated system, which combines imaging, enterprise content management, and intranet strategies into one cohesive organizational initiative.
- Limiting imaging and content management to departments with ample funding may restrict these technologies from being used in the areas where they are needed most.

In paper- or microfilm-based environments, customer service response is often very slow because of the time required to retrieve information. Sometimes, paper documents cannot be found because they have been misfiled or lost. The result is a dissatisfied customer, and ultimately, the loss of business, money, and time. Typical imaging installations have realized the following benefits:

- 25–50% increase in transactions per employee.
- 30–40% reduction in clerical staff.
- 50–80% reduction in storage space.
- 100% reduction in transaction time.

Imaging Capture Center Operations

Organizations considering imaging projects should also consider whether to build a centralized imaging conversion center. This is a

very important consideration because of the significant cost repre-
sented by both the creation of an imaging conversion center and the
use of outsourcing. Also, when building processes for which senior
management is responsible, it is important to measure the risk of all
of the options. Before discussing the differences between internal or
external capture services, the components and terminology of the
imaging conversion process are examined.

Conversion and Capture

Inventorying is the process of assessing the paper files, file types and
usage patterns of the paper documents. Scanning is the process of
converting an input document to a digitally stored image that can be
displayed on a workstation screen. Scanning and inventorying combined with indexing are the key components of an imaging conversion system. Input documents may be one or more sheets of paper,
facsimiles in digital form or paper, computer-based files like Word
documents, photographs captured by digital cameras, or even signa-
tures captured by digital signature pads.

Once an image is scanned and stored ("captured"), it can be
displayed, printed, faxed, exported, or archived. Using the image
viewer, the imaged documents can be re-indexed, annotated, zoomed
in or out, or rotated depending on the end user's needs. Conversion
from paper-based filing to an imaging system requires significant
planning.

The term *indexing* refers to the addition of metadata to a image
file. The index facilitates the retrieval of electronic files by giving them
searchable properties. While an imaging system provides much faster
retrieval of documents (a financial benefit), the mere availability of a
new technology does not justify its acquisition. The real measure of
value should be whether the solution fixes an important organizational problem and improves the overall business process.

Effective indexing can add value to a process far beyond improving the speed of retrieval. Good metadata indexes enable users to
retrieve documents in many different ways. Think of organizational
records as part of a hierarchy of "containers" that includes levels
such as folder, section, document, and page. A folder can have many
sections, sections can contain many documents, and documents can
consist of many pages. Yet traditional paper-based filing systems

require users to retrieve all information at the folder level of the hierarchy. By contrast, imaging systems allow information to be retrieved at many levels. This flexible retrieval capability is built on the metadata indexing, which is the bedrock of imaging. The accurate and consistent indexing of digital records is absolutely critical to the success of any imaging system.

The cost of imaging conversion and capture is typically based on several factors, including the following:

- Document size.
- Document prep labor costs for removing staples and sticky notes attached to them.
- Document sorting labor costs, prior to scanning.
- Paper type and color.
- Single-sided paper or double-sided scanning (simplex or duplex).
- Optical character recognition/intelligent character recognition (OCR/ICR) costs versus labor savings.
- The number and length of indexes to be entered.
- Document reassembly labor costs.

Because of the differences in imaging options, it is important to build common abstractions on which the customer and capture provider can agree. Metadata serve as a document container that facilitates retrieval and reuse of content. The following are examples of simple categories that can be used as a basis for bidding and building imaging projects:

- *Box-level imaging.* This represents a low-cost imaging solution that indexes metadata at the container level. A single set of metadata properties serves for as many as 2000 pages. The cost of this type of capture is around 7–9 cents per page. This product was designed to be a replacement for microfiche and provide cheap, simple document retention suitable for rarely retrieved images.
- *Folder-level imaging.* This solution is designed to capture documents that are accessed only occasionally. Like recreating filing cabinets in electronic form, document images are indexed with the same information that would appear at the top of file folders. Folder-level indexing brings the basic flexibility and

mobility of imaging while keeping costs low. It offers a higher level of indexing for approximately 20 cents per page.

■ *Full-service imaging.* Companies may need a higher level of searchable metadata for documents that are retrieved often. Comparable to a desk drawer, full-service imaging places the most often retrieved documents at any number of users' fingertips. Full-service imaging usually includes more advanced services, such as data proofing, advanced sorting, full text indexing, optical character recognition, or intelligent character recognition.

These services begin at the document level of indexing and move upward in complexity and cost. They typically require custom bids; and the price varies depending on project size, location, and specifications.

Provided next is a description of the staff of an average imaging conversion center. This should help you better understand what resources are required to manage an imaging project and conversion on a continuous basis. Most imaging conversion centers have a variety of team member roles that are essential for sustainable success. These are the most common roles found in an imaging conversion center:

■ The *department manager* provides vision, leadership, and strategic direction for the entire department. The manager also enforces policies and oversees training, budgeting, and resource investments. Typically, the manager also participates in the bidding for new customers and selling of large imaging conversion projects.

■ The *project managers* provide leadership and facilitate logistical support to conversion projects. They also promote imaging throughout the enterprise and deliver detailed, customized bids and products to customers.

■ The *system administrators* could be separate from the department or housed within the imaging conversion center. Their main duties include technical support of the imaging system, security, and account management; they also may help with the bulk loading of data.

■ The *analysts* manage development of small projects, document procedures, supervise interns, research best practices, and perform low-level customization and configuration of existing systems and testing of new technologies. They also meet with customers to define new procedures and products that support the customer's goals.

- The *project coordinators* duties include team leadership, maintaining existing customer relationships, providing critical appraisal of indexing employee output, and training new imaging clerks. This position also provides a promotion path for imaging clerks.

- *Imaging clerks* (half organizational employees, half temporary employees) operate scanning or indexing workstations, perform basic clerical functions, physically move paper documents to be converted, enter metadata into indexes, and check records for data integrity. Over time, they develop a strong understanding of the nature of their customer's documents and how customers' retrieval needs change.

In-House or Outsourced

Because of the number of options that can be included with any imaging project, it is very important to have some expertise in-house, regardless of whether the actual work is outsourced. It is very easy to overpay on an imaging project, because of the complexity of the decisions and negotiations the project manager makes. The project tasks and procedural enforcement issues look different between in-house and outsourced data capture, but in either case, those responsibilities still chiefly lie with the project manager.

Look at the differences in responsibilities listed in Tables 9.2 and 9.3. First, we examine outsourced data capture. Regardless of whether the actual document conversion work is outsourced, the responsibility stays with the organization. Table 9.3 examines the responsibility in an in-house conversion.

When considering a large, back-file imaging conversion of documents, weighing the options is important. However, any organization considering imaging documents should realize that that it cannot outsource the responsibility for managing the conversion process. Because of this, many organizations choose to build internal departments that handle large back-file conversions and smaller point-forward conversions.

Table 9.2

Responsibility in an Outsourced Conversion Project

Task	Organization's Responsibility?	Outsourcer's Responsibility?
Define the scope of the imaging project	Yes	Yes
Define the document retention period	Yes	No
Define the type of documents and their proper indexing	Yes	Yes
Define and manage an outsourcing contract	Yes	Yes
Manage the transportation of the documents	Yes	Yes
Manage the conversion of the documents	No	Yes
Quality assurance and validity check	Yes	Yes
Load the converted images into the production system	Yes	Yes
Determine the success of the conversion project	Yes	Yes

Table 9.3

Responsibilities When Using an Internal Conversion Center

Task	Departmental Project Manager's Responsibility?	Internal Conversion Center's Responsibility?
Define the scope of the imaging project	Yes	Yes
Define the document retention period	Yes	No
Define the type of documents and their proper indexing	Yes	Yes
Manage the transportation of the documents	No, unless requires leaving a campus	Yes
Manage the conversion of the documents	No	Yes
Quality assurance and validity check	Yes	Yes
Load the converted images into the production system	No	Yes
Determine the success of the conversion project	Yes	Yes

Another key consideration is cost and efficiency. The outsourced model is built on the idea that the outsourcer has created an organization large enough to handle large back-file conversions and its overall efficiency provides a cost advantage. Basically, its efficiency offsets the markup on its services. This makes it reasonable for an organization to consider sending the work off-site.

Some organizations handle the document conversion offshore, and others actually use the state prison systems for cheap labor. However, these organizations also have to accept an increase in the risk of losing certain documents and the cost of moving the data back to the organization and loading it into the content management system. Also, the company hiring convicts to handle customer records, risks a public relations nightmare.

One key advantage of internal conversion centers is that documents typically do not leave the organizational campus to be scanned. This can be important for several legal and regulatory reasons. Another advantage is that the documents are loaded into the system on a daily basis, not as part of a large bulk load. This means that the internal customer can almost immediately begin viewing the results of the imaging work and determine quickly whether the conversion department is properly sorting, indexing, and scanning the documents.

The time delay that typically happens with an outsourced conversion shop can also mean that work progresses for several days or even weeks before a problem is caught. Once a problem is caught, it typically means that the organization's project manager and a managing representative of the outsourcing conversion shop must reach a compromise solution. Often, this requires an amount of rework that grows in relation to the time delay.

You need to understand the difference between outsourcing task items and outsourcing an entire business process. For example, outsourcing invoice scanning and indexing (document conversion) to improve the Accounts Payables Department's efficiency is completely different than moving the accounts payables process to an outsource provider.

The first example is delegation; and for every scanning or indexing error, the customer's project manager spends the time to make corrections. In contrast, outsourcing the entire A/P process means that, if errors occur, a manager's time is spent correcting the process at the departmental product level, which is much more cost effective.

Outsourcing an entire process, back-file, and point forward conversions through a network linked, outsourcing provider solution is often very feasible. Organizations such as IBM, Xerox, and Kodak provide process outsourcing that includes imaging conversion. In most cases, the decision to build an internal imaging conversion shop versus outsourcing to an outside provider is made based on the age old question of whether the organization wishes to amortize a capital investment over the next few years or record the cost this year as an expense.

In-House Imaging Conversion Services

The first area examined is in-house imaging conversion services. If the imaging conversion is handled by an internal imaging center, many other internal services might be offered. One service that is typically very important to Human Relation Departments is job resume conversion and management. Managing the shared resume databases that support recruiting for an organization can be challenging, but it can also be very important for company success. Resume handling services are very expensive; and by converting all of the resumes into digital documents and sharing them throughout an organization, paper consumption is reduced, recruiters' time is saved, and the overall cost for hiring is reduced.

Another reason for building an internal imaging department is the expertise that becomes available when looking to increase efficiency in any department affected by the flow of paper documents. Imaging is an enabling technology, and when coupled with workflow, it can strongly leverage an organization's people and processes. Many times, the need is not only the long-term storage of paper documents but also the ability to transfer documents electronically as part of an automated work process.

Corporate recruiters are constantly handling resumes, either receiving and reviewing them or forwarding them to potential hiring managers. Many times the resume is included in a workflow, where the hiring manager's thoughts and opinions about a candidate can also be recorded. This type of feedback is often lost if the hiring manager uses a paper resume, because those comments are handwritten on the resume copy instead of a comments field in the recruiting system. Imaging systems can also help to prevent the embarrassing situation where two recruiters from the same company compete for the same candidate.

Although this type of process management can be handled by an outsource provider, smaller groups typically ask the personnel to manage the relationship with outside providers. Internal services can often be promoted throughout the organizational communication streams, allowing small departments to understand their value and availability.

Centralization and Decentralization of Imaging Conversion

Data capture strategies should be looked at on a project-by-project basis by the supporting project teams to determine whether or not to employ centralized capture. If the volume of pages to be converted reaches an amount that merits a new centralized capture center being built in another location, the original capture centers procedures and specifications can be implemented to save time and money. Centralized and decentralized capture are discussed further in Chapter 3.

FUNDING THROUGH SARBANES-OXLEY COMPLIANCE

In recent years, the all too common cover story has been "Auditors Uncovered Evidence of an Even Wider Fraud," then the eventual collapse of the organization and the arrest of the key executives. What happened to the improved organizational vision that information technologies was suppose to enable? Did the executives have a clear understanding of what was happening in their organization? Good business processes manage the handling and monitoring of data, but keep in mind that technology has its limits.

The world economy has reeled from the accusations of multibillion dollar fraud at organizations like Andersen, Enron, and WorldCom. Because of the negative effects of the faltering organizations on Wall Street, a large number of regulations have begun falling on businesses. This change in the business climate has affected not only the U.S. market but European businesses as well.

The most prominent of these new regulations is the Sarbanes-Oxley Act of 2002, which many lay claim to being the most important legislation governing public companies since the establishment of the Securities and Exchange Commission (SEC) in 1934. With all the new business regulation, the big question is: How will companies comply?

Lawmakers have begun applying pressure for businesses to keep accurate records and document internal revenue processes and controls. Without the right expertise and available IT systems, success seems impossible. Whether the job is achievable or not, IT executives are quickly being hit with questions about direction in this issue. IT must develop or purchase the architecture to face these new challenges. None of this has been lost on the IT industry, which is desperate for new sources of growth. Many companies are driving forward with implementations of their products as businesses begin racing to conform.

Since the initiation of the Sarbanes-Oxley Act of 2002, companies like FileNet, IBM, Oracle, PeopleSoft, Kodak, Clearswift, Hyperion, Citicus, and BoardVantage began offering products to help business executives with their regulator requirements. Most of these are existing tools that have been enhanced and refocused. The original tools used a variety of technologies, including performance management, enterprise resource planning, document management, content management, and e-mail management applications.

Many organizations fear that the scare around these new regulations will overshadow other initiatives. The job of helping the organization set priorities often falls to the project managers. Project managers need to work very closely with the executive team, which must be able to understand and act on the statistical information provided them. Without their understanding of the business, the metrics mean nothing.

Beyond the overload of information is the control of information at the top of organizations. Where does the buck stop? It may not stop until it reaches the board of directors. This means some shake-ups in how information moves up the chain. Too often, the board is not operating with the information needed to make sound decisions. This has to change before Wall Street can bounce back.

The big question now being asked is: Can the organizations afford to make these changes? Recent surveys found that more than 75% of organizations spend more on IT infrastructure and consulting services as a direct result of the Sarbanes-Oxley Act of 2002, but many of those organizations are concerned that they may not be able to conform quickly enough and their original estimates were low.

Technical costs are not the only costs businesses face; there are also the costs of financial audits to make sure the new systems and procedures meet the requirements. Recent surveys have set expectations for Sarbanes-Oxley compliance at 5000–10,000 hours and $500,000–1 million to complete the task. Many software companies believe this to be an opportunity second only to the pre-Y2K software and services buying spree.

Regardless of these costs, CFOs must certify that their companies' financial statements are accurate. They must also demonstrate that their internal financial controls and processes produce accurate results. Failure to comply with the Sarbanes-Oxley Act of 2002 could cost some CFOs their wealth and freedom.

FileNet/Steelpoint Offering

FileNet joined compliance and risk management specialist Steelpoint Technologies to design a solution to aid in the compliance of Sarbanes-Oxley Act of 2002. FileNet with its existing expertise in enterprise content management and business process management technologies and Steelpoint's Introspect litigation support application are well aligned to quickly enter the Sarbanes-Oxley support software foray. At the core of their software solution is Steelpoint's eDiscovery product, which enables organizations to capture, index, and store content from many sources. The product also aids in identifying relevant content and the collaboration on risk issues. The combination of the two corporations' efforts has been the development of a compliance and litigation risk management (CLRM) solution.

The partnership does not stop with the Sarbanes-Oxley Act of 2002 but is designed to help organizations manage risk and comply with a wide range of corporate governance requirements and regulations. Also in the scope of this new offering is the Health Insurance Portability and Accountability Act and the U.S. Patriot Act, as well as a many environmental and government antitrust regulations.

A few of the companies offering software and services to deal with Sarbanes-Oxley Act of 2002 are FileNet, IBM, Oracle, PeopleSoft, Kodak, Clearswift, Hyperion, Citicus, BoardVantage, Nth Orbit, and Cognos.

Other regulatory compliance issues on the horizon include Basel II and IAS 2005. Also known as the New Basel Capital Accord, Basel

II is an updated global code of conduct for information risk-management that financial institutions must comply with by the end of 2006. European companies must consolidate their financial reports in agreement with International Accounting Standards (IAS) by 2005 under a European Union directive.

SUCCESS STORY

A financial services company, with offices in 20 countries worldwide, generates thousands of pages of computer reports everyday. Over time, managing this mountain of reports became progressively less efficient. The company is faced with the need to provide secure access, for auditors and accountants, to customer transactions. These transactions need to be maintained for many years in a system that provides quick access, regardless of the age of the document. The system has to be extremely reliable and compliant with strict SEC regulations.

After examining the requirements and needs of the company, FileNet's Report Manager tool was chosen because of the flexibility of its user interface and its ability to scale into an enterprisewide ECM solution. To meet the mission-critical nature of this implementation, two servers were used (primary and fail-over).

The benefits include the following:

- Quick access to reports.
- Data mining capabilities.
- Savings of $150,000 per year over paper and microfiche.
- Elimination of paper handling costs (printing, copying, and distribution).
- Improved problem resolution.
- Reduced re-keying of information across multiple legacy systems.

Chapter 10

FILENET, KNOWLEDGE MANAGEMENT, AND LEADERSHIP

Leadership is lifting a person's vision to higher sights, raising a person's performance beyond its normal limitations.

—Peter Drucker

KEY OBJECTIVES

- Learn how FileNet can help organizations automate their processes, provide better connectivity throughout the organization, and integrate existing processes and applications.
- Understand FileNet's potential to support organizational knowledge management initiatives.
- Understand how enterprise content management can improve attention management and organizational decision making.
- Gain an awareness of how documents can help to balance competing objectives by identifying potential solutions, making

176

them explicit, and helping groups reach acceptable levels of consensus.

■ Understand why the intelligent management of documents is a key component in empowering companies to harness the ideas and innovativeness of their employees.

■ Catch a glimpse of future enterprise content management systems.

PROCESSES AND INTEGRATION

Humans are skilled in making judgments about complex subjects; computers are designed to follow procedures strictly. An organization's computer systems should be used to prevent mundane tasks from using up the individual employee's attention and ensure that processes requiring strict procedural compliance are automated to the highest degree possible.

Currently, many products are designed to integrate processes and exchange information to enable effective workflow. These content management tools are changing businesses by removing the top-down hierarchies previously required to manage processes.

FileNet's Business Process Manager and the other products in their application suite were designed to compete in this very competitive market by providing predictable results and stability.

Organizations that typically need this type of toolset are:

■ Businesses whose processes have become unpredictable.

■ Departments and organizations that have complex, interrelated processes.

■ Organizations suffering with disconnected systems and information barriers.

■ Groups fragmented by distributed locations and time zones, leading to sluggish tactical decision making.

■ Companies bound to well-established manual environments with strong resistance to changes in the status quo.

Automating business processes can build predictability into processes, but organizations also need tools from which to build metrics that help project future business. FileNet's Business Process Manager (BPM) uses OLAP (On-Line Analytical Processing) technology for data analysis. The data cubes it creates allow "slicing and dicing" the data to interactively explore data from different perspectives.

FileNet's Business Process Manager, along with its suite of content managing applications, can help organizations automate their processes, provide connectivity throughout the organization, integrate existing processes and applications, as well as provide connectivity for future endeavors. To be successful, project managers must ensure that the correct set of FileNet components is chosen for implementation. If all the required components are not implemented, custom programming could be required to make the business process work. If more components are implemented than actually needed, there is a risk of project cost overruns and excess complexity.

Enterprise Content Management Components

An organization hoping to move into ECM should first establish clear business objectives and process documentation. Use investigation, analysis, and dialog to determine what organizational information flow problems exist and whether a proposed solution will actually solve those issues. An organization needs to understand the components of an ECM solution. Figure 10.1 provides a glimpse of the typical ECM components and how they integrate together. Understanding what ECM solutions offer begins the development of a new abstraction that includes new ideas, terminologies, and solutions.

The following is a general list of components found in typical ECM systems. Remember that each vendor will try to convince your organization that the component in which it is strongest is the key component to solve your organization's problems. Do not be misled, arm yourself with as much knowledge as possible before even contacting any vendor companies.

- ■ *Document imaging.* These are applications designed for scanning, indexing, retrieving, and archiving digital images and managing metadata. Images could be of paper text, graphics, engineering drawings, or photographs. The better imaging systems also include powerful workflow engines to assure that paper is not only converted but that the new images become part of the accountability and workflow of an organization.

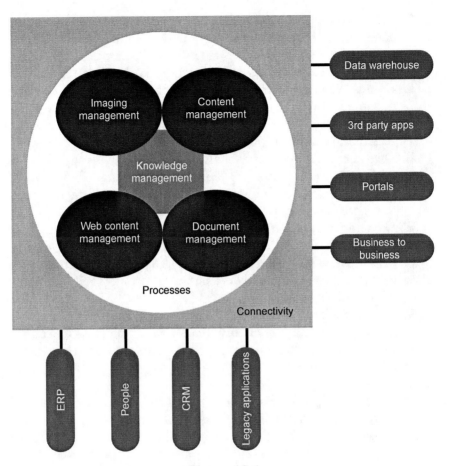

Figure 10.1
Enterprise content management

- *COLD/EDI* (Computer Output to Laser Disk and Electronic Document Interchange). These applications are designed to manage high-volume computer-generated reports and data archiving. Some provide components for data mining and form formatting to reprint the data in its original format.
- *Records management.* Applications of this type are for managing long-term document archives and document life cycles. This typically includes the documented, systematic, storage and eventual destruction of documents, both paper and electronic.

- *Web content management.* These applications manage the capture, presentation, delivery, and maintenance of online objects, including documents and graphics for the primary purpose of disseminating information via the Web.
- *Document management.* These applications manage electronic documents through the building of metadata to allow collaboration, revision control, annotations, workflow, and connection to retention applications and processes.
- *Digital asset management.* DAM applications manage the life cycle of large collections of digital assets, such as photographic images, graphics, brand logos, and compound documents. They focus on maximizing effective reuse of digital objects.
- *Content integration* (content federation). These middleware applications integrate multiple vendor repositories.
- *Media asset management.* A subset of DAM, MAM is specific to rich media, such as video and audio, that require complex management tools.
- *Collaboration tools.* Any of several applications that promote groups working together effectively. Typical applications include project workspaces, project management tools, automated reporting tools, and basic workflow.

When an organization has documented its issues and become acquainted with the major enterprise content manager products, it is ready to set the project scope and begin taking bids. Once the scope has been set, most companies issue a request for proposals (RFP) document. If ECM solutions are new to the organization, research should include obtaining process roadmaps from several ECM vendors. These process roadmaps delineate the integration of disparate content technologies from beginning to end.

Choosing FileNet

FileNet is a widely recognized leader in document imaging and the production workflow field, and it has competitive COLD and document management products. FileNet has seen the ECM field emerge and reengineered and rebranded its product lines for document imaging, Web content management, document management, workflow, and business process management.

The FileNet P8 product line includes Business Process Manager, FileNet Content Manager (document management, low-volume imaging, and workflow), FileNet Web Content Manager, FileNet Image Manager (high-volume imaging and workflow), and FileNet Forms Manager. These products are available for .NET and J2EE platforms, with the exception of FileNet Image Manager, which is Microsoft centered. FileNet's J2EE products are built on a business process management foundation and offer event-driven architecture and life cycle management for both process and content, portal integration, and business process simulation.

FileNet recently strengthened its ECM offerings with the purchase of the Web content management vendor eGrail and e-forms vendor Shana. These purchases demonstrate its focus on managing active content. FileNet considers "active content" to be documents that can launch processes like retrieving and distributing content, exception handling, initiating queries, or automating approvals. An order document could be thought of as active content because it kicks off the sales process. The active content focus will continue to be critical as organizations attempt to comply with regulations like Sarbanes-Oxley Act of 2002, Department of Defense 5015.2, Securities and Exchange Commission 17 CFR 240 17A-4, CFR 21 CFR Part 11, HIPAA, and emerging regulations from the Environmental Protection Agency and the Patent and Trademark Office.

Good Leaders Value Attention

An organization that values knowledge management works to ensure that learning occurs before, during, and after any major event or project. A variety of procedural, technological, and cultural tools are used to support those goals. KM is not simply the toolset used to pursue the goals but also the philosophy of valuing the attention of other people and appreciating the diversity of opinions and experiences they offer. In fact, most experts agree that learning is essentially a social process. This means that the most valuable KM initiatives usually address the culture rather than focus blindly on the technological infrastructure. However, it is important to note that organizations with a focus on the value of KM place a premium on the sound management of their employee's attention.

Attention Management Issues FileNet Can Help Address

- Developing workflows that build in information sharing and unbiased performance metrics.
- Providing technological integration points that support and automate information sharing and collaboration while mitigating geographical distances.
- Providing transparent, easily accessible repositories for mission critical content that values the attention of users.
- Engaging management and business process leaders to work more closely with IT in planning projects, setting policy, identifying opportunities, and analyzing risks.
- Developing, formalizing, and distributing strong procedures for evolutionary improvement of critical business processes.

Often KM consulting groups spend a great deal of time arguing over whether an IT system manages information or knowledge. Since most documents can represent knowledge to one employee and information to another, this activity is not especially helpful. In fact, information hoarding is as popular as knowledge hoarding, and corporate employees are provided many incentives to avoid admitting ignorance of anything.

As the organization changes over time, finding something as simple as the phone number for a process owner can become a nearly impossible task. Workflow systems like FileNet allow for automating information sharing behind the scenes. This means the information provider has no chance to refuse sharing the information, and the information consumer is not forced to admit ignorance. This transparency drastically reduces the amount of trust required to effectively collaborate, and trust is a very rare, valuable resource in any company—smart businesses use it accordingly.

To a large extent, KM is about finding new ways to encourage and facilitate openness within an organization. In an environment that does not value transparency, ideas are filtered by command rather than dialog. Ideas cultivated in this environment tend to yield a crop of unchecked assumptions and bad practices. Culture is important to KM strategies, because the filtering of ideas is much too difficult to automate. The only effective filter for ideas is a dynamic dialog among a diverse group of stakeholders.

Transparency Improves Both Vision and Judgment

A dialog among a diverse group of stakeholders can deliver two key benefits: far-reaching vision and sound judgment. Most company executives agree these are two of the most important assets a company must have to be successful. They may even tell you that these two critical assets are what they "bring to the party." No technology vendor pitches these two deliverables in its statement of work. Vision and judgment are beyond the ability of any technology ever created, and no one wants to pitch automating the boss' job anyway.

However, it would be short-sighted to assume that vision and judgment are solely the domain of managers. Humans have two eyes because each eyes receives only two-dimensional retina images with no special component for depth perception. However, clear and accurate vision is obtained by seeing an image from multiple points of view and examining the differences between the two images. Similarly, the accuracy, completeness, and value of the knowledge and learning in the organization will always depend on the full and informed participation of the stakeholders.

Balancing Competing Objectives

An active, informed dialog is critical for dealing with conflicts caused by competing objectives. In any partnership, team, or organization conflict is bound to arise between members who do not see eye to eye. The issue is not so much about who is right and who is wrong but how to successfully work together when efforts contradict one another.

For instance, a company hires a worker hoping to gain an efficient employee that will improve the productivity of the business and save money. The worker goes to work for the company to make as much income as he or she can. On the simplest level, these objectives are in competition. When dealing with complex issues, competing objectives are more the rule than the exception.

During the years leading to the American Revolutionary War, not everyone in the colonies was excited by the idea of self-rule. Many citizens believed that common men were not intelligent enough to participate in ruling the country. They believed that a society of noble people should control the affairs of state and the common man should know his place in the order of things. Even after the Revolution, a similar argument was raised with regard to states rights.

States-rights proponents felt that individual states should govern themselves with a loose confederation to bind them together. At the same time, many advocated the need for a stronger federal government to protect the rights of individuals. The southern states were even willing to go to war over this issue. The southern states feared the power that was being centralized into the hands of a few powerful federal leaders. However, their solution was to centralize power into the hands of the planters, the nobility of the South.

Whenever a group of people unites to achieve something, a structure of rules and expectations are created. In some cases, the rules that balance the rights and expectations of the individual with the goals of the group are explicitly defined, such as in a constitution. In other cases, the structure is informal and unspoken, such as so-called pecking orders. In any case, there is a dynamic tension between the individual's need for liberty and the group's need to achieve its objectives and sustain the survival of the group itself.

For people to function in groups, some collective decisions must be made that are generally regarded as binding on the group and enforced as common policy. A constitution explicitly details how to balance the competing objectives between the individual citizen and the population as a whole. The rules may not be perfect, but they are widely available to the group's members and open to review.

Groups that are formed without this explicit documentation of the group's structure are *not* without structure. Interactions between groups of people *always* have a structure, but many have informal structures or combinations of formal and informal structures. Making the process for balancing the competing objectives of the individual and group explicit is an important part of ensuring the success and long-term sustainability of the group.

Today's companies face a wide range of competing objectives, but the fundamental issue is the conflict between dialog and direction. Companies desperately need a rich diversity of dialog to ensure that best practices remain "best." However, often dialog can stymie efforts to respond quickly to a changing situation. When the business climate changes suddenly, an organization's leader must be able to rapidly direct the actions of the workforce, with the full expectation of timely compliance.

The new battlefield for the confrontation between dialog and direction is the organization, company, or corporation. How does the organization allow authoring of ideas to their knowledge bases or innovation databases? Do only the "stars" ideas get accepted into these information repositories? Have they created a "knowledge nobility"?

This is critical to understand because businesses in the United States are at a crossroads. Do they move forward into the Information Age, where the individual's attention is the currency, or stay in the Industrial Age, with the hierarchy of control that was instituted by the rail barons of the nineteenth century? Ultimately, the answer is in our decision-making processes.

DECISION-MAKING PROCESSES

When teams work on complex tasks that require judgment, it is often useful to "decide how to decide." Developing a group constitution is one way for a group to reach consensus on the issue of deciding how to decide. Decision analysis techniques use specialized documents to help decision makers clarify problems and separate facts from priorities and preferences. Unfortunately, attempts to obtain objectivity are often thwarted by measurement difficulties, problem complexity, or time constraints.

The issue of competing objectives is so prevalent that a number of decision aid tools have been developed to help mitigate these types of issues. The utilization of decision aid tools can significantly improve the decision-making process in terms of efficiency, efficacy, and transparency. Although there are numerous decision aid tools, for this chapter, the focus is on two: multiple criteria decision analysis (MCDA) and the nominal group technique (NGT).

Multiple Criteria Decision Analysis

The MCDA technique evolved from the field of economic theory. The technique consists of applying mathematical modeling in an attempt to support decision making involving trade-offs. The problems it addresses generally involve choosing one of a number of alternatives based on how well those alternatives rate against a previously defined set of criteria. The criteria are weighted in terms of importance to the stakeholders and the overall "score" of an alternative is the weighted sum of its rating against each criteria. Through ordering the alternatives by their decision scores, a preference ranking is derived.

Balancing competing objectives via categorization and ranking like this involves managing three key issues: uncertainty regarding what is known and unknown, motivations and values associated with objectives, and the options or alternatives from which to choose. The process consists of developing value criteria with stakeholders, measurement guidelines with experts, and then ranking the alternatives. In the end, the result is a matrix as exampled in Table 10.1.

Even though this technique often appears to be 90% defining the problem and 10% finding the answer; the key benefit is in improved understanding, communication, and a greater sense of shared mission among team members. One of the biggest risks in using multiple criteria decision analysis is that group participation is low, leading to weighting bias in the various scales used to balance the objectives. The nominal group technique, discussed next, is a variation of MCDA devised to improve group participation in the decision-making process.

Nominal Group Technique

Most experts agree that 50–80% of the typical manager's time is spent in meetings. Sadly, most managers feel that much of this time

Table 10.1
Multiple Criteria Decision Analysis Matrix

Options	Response	Flexibility	Mobility	Service	Ease
Option 1	3	8	5	7	7
Option 2	5	4	7	5	8
Option 3	10	3	10	3	10
Option 4	5.5	5	7	5	5
Option 5	3	10	5	10	3
Option 6	3	6	5	6	2
Total	29.5	36	39	36	35
Weight	10	5	2	10	5

is wasted. Teams (that are often teams only in name) trying to generate ideas and encourage active member involvement while maintaining agendas and time schedules encounter many problems. Too often, certain team members are excluded from active participation.

In other situations, discussions are controlled by a subset of the team's members. As the meeting progresses, everyone either talks or listens; and there is no time for people to think through the issues. The team strives for impartiality, consistency, and objectivity in its decision making; however, the more outside views that are allowed into the group, the more difficult it is to make sure these ideas are shared. The rationality of the objectives is neither necessary nor sufficient for the attainment of success. Research in the field of group dynamics indicates that more ideas are expressed by individuals working alone in a group environment than those expressed by individuals engaged in a formal group discussion.

To address these collaboration issues, Andrew Delbecq and Andrew Van de Ven created the nominal group technique. NGT is similar to brainstorming, but it uses a more structured format to obtain multiple inputs from several people on a particular problem or issue. Individuals, working alone then later in groups, brainstorm ideas using procedures that encourage creativity and discourage criticism and evaluation.

The name *nominal group technique* attempts to make it clear that, in the beginning, a team is that in name only. It takes time and effort to create a team that shares common abstractions and balanced objectives. Until then, it is merely a named (nominal) group. A team shares common abstractions and has worked to balance the competing objectives. Being part of a demographic (program users, Web programmers, marketing managers, and so on) does not make one part of a team. Teams are interdependent.

The NGT seeks to build a matrix similar to MCDA, but extra measures are taken to encourage creativity and discourage the early criticism and evaluation that often lead to low levels of group participation. Typically, participants not only produce more ideas when working alone but do so without sacrificing quality. Too often, people fail to actively participate in a team because they fear they'll look foolish or stupid; therefore, they censor themselves. The following is a high-level overview of the NGT process:

1. Individuals generate ideas privately during or before the team meeting.

2. The ideas are collected and listed on a whiteboard or a piece of paper.
3. Each person takes a turn reading one of his or her ideas in a round-robin fashion.
4. The group discusses the ideas on the list, possibly adding new ideas as they go.
5. Each group member ranks the listed ideas.
6. Individual rankings are summarized for each idea to form a group ranking.
7. The group ranking of ideas is discussed in an attempt to arrive at a consensus.
8. If the group ranking is unacceptable and consensus cannot be achieved, repeat steps 3 through 6.

The technique can be very time consuming, and group size is a critical issue. Typically, group size should be seven to nine people. Eleven people is the absolute maximum, so larger groups should be divided into groups of seven to nine for the process. It is quite difficult for most people to keep from discussing issues before all the points are listed, clarified, and ranked. So, the meeting facilitator must take care to prevent the discussion phase from starting too early in the process. Properly conducted, the NGT leads to better decisions with much higher levels of team buy-in.

Do Not Discount the Value of Documents

Multiple criteria decision analysis tools and nominal group technique exercises have in common the use documents to identify potential solutions, make them explicit, and help a group reach an acceptable level of consensus. These decision aid tools use documents not simply to capture knowledge and make it explicit but to actively aid in thinking and enabling dialog within a team. Further research will lead to a wealth of examples of documents that facilitate communication and dialog in corporate settings.

Documents help mitigate the frailty of human memory as well as ensure common understandings that support shared meaning. They also help improve employee accountability by mitigating the confusion caused by he said/she said conflicts. Documents have long been the glue that holds organizations together. They support decisions, aid in communication, and provide the critical information infrastructure for almost every business process. This is why the intelligent management of documents is a key component in empowering companies to harness the ideas and innovativeness of their employees.

A few companies have recognized the need to embrace the individuals within their organizations and harness their ideas. IBM has many internal programs for rewarding individual and teams that share their ideas. One program, mentioned earlier in this text, empowers individual employees to give gifts of IBM logo-bearing merchandise to others within the organization for appreciation and sharing of ideas. IBM also spends attention meeting with individuals that author to their innovation databases. These types of activities are important steps in harnessing the vast knowledge and strength of an organization's individual workers.

Attention, Analysis, and Dialog

This text has made a point to drive home the importance of attention to the individual and the organization. As stated before, *attention is the currency of the Information Age.* Organizational leaders that do not value the attention of their employees risk wasting their most vital resource.

Because of the importance of attention, it is vital that individuals and organizations effectively manage the attention they give and receive. To often, Communications Departments fail to get representation on company projects. In the end, these departments risk presenting an image of the organization that sets a false expectation or is just plain wrong.

Getting internal feedback can often be critical in stopping a possible "black eye." The 2003 public relations ad campaign for the city of Hong Kong was to be based on the phrase, "Come to Hong Kong, We Will Take Your Breath Away." This would have been a complete disaster in light of the 2003 outbreak of the respiratory illness SARS. Luckily, someone noticed the problem and the campaign was changed, much to the relief of the Hong Kong leaders—and to the detriment of an army of stand-up comics around the world.

Norman Vincent Peale said, "The trouble with most of us is that we would rather be ruined by praise than saved by criticism." If attention is the currency, then analysis is the accounting of the Information Age. What good is attention if results are not analyzed to determine patterns? Every system generates information, some of which leaves the system. We all regularly send information to other systems, and we receive information from them. Feedback from another system often enables us to evaluate our services and to make them more self-renewing.

A feedback loop represents the pattern of interacting processes, where a change in one variable, through interaction with other variables in the system, either reinforces the original process (positive feedback) or suppresses it (negative feedback). Feedback loops occur whenever part of an output of some system is connected back into one of its inputs. Lack of frequent useful feedback is a leading negative influence on worker performance. Implementing feedback loops that encompass the whole supply chain, as in Figure 10.2, within a workflow offers a cost-effective intervention solution that rapidly leads to improved performance.

In the end, dialog must happen, because regardless of the graphs, databases, or spreadsheets created from the information gathered, the complexity of our world requires human judgment assess its value and relevance. This is why conversations are the cornerstone of all business operations.

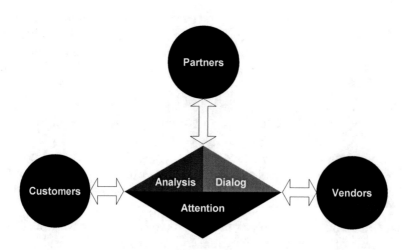

Figure 10.2
Attention, analysis, and dialog

The Unique Characteristics of Conversation

Conversation has always been considered essential to business. In fact, it is the key medium for learning and decision making. The mere presentation of information does not necessarily result in learning or action. People have to become actively involved for behavior to change, insight to occur, and problems to be solved. The unique characteristics of conversation make it the ideal way to get people actively involved in problem solving:

1. *Conversation is dynamic.* In conversation we notice how our audience is reacting. The pace of communication is slowed or advanced based on listener needs, speaker objectives, and even surrounding events. These needs are indicated subtly through eye contact, head nodding, questions, facial expressions, fidgeting—even heckling. These dynamic characteristics of human conversations make them incredibly flexible and powerful for solving problems.

2. *Conversation is personalized.* In conversations, we instinctively refer to already established understandings, shared memories, and past history. We tailor our language to inform without offending, to inquire without interrogating, and to balance advocacy with inquiry. This personalization improves the chances of reaching shared meaning and consensus.

3. *Conversation is self-correcting.* When misunderstandings occur in conversations, we attempt to fix them by creating new metaphors, defining our terms, rephrasing our words, and the like. Active listeners provide both verbal and nonverbal cues to confirm their understanding (or lack of) of complex topics. The self-correcting nature of conversation often prevents the major communication breakdowns that come from differing abstractions.

The best document management systems of the future will not only allow documents to be stored but enable people to converse with one another and exchange viewpoints using the documents to provide clear context and long-term persistence to the conversation. Such a system would capture things like user reviews of documents, retrieval counts, user activity-level assessments, and even disputing opinions and information. It would integrate content management, searching, collaboration, and learning to enable an endless cycle of business process improvement.

Knowledge management is not simply a matter of archiving and distributing information. However, it is also more complicated than simply setting aside more time for storytelling around the water cooler. FileNet products are robust enough to vastly improve the way a company manages the attention of it workers, and for many companies, that is where KM begins.

CONCLUSION

Globalization and changing corporate regulations are altering the business landscape and will continue to drive the enterprise content management business forward for the next few years. The result is an evolving understanding by organizations that they need control of their content and the processes that go into creating that content. This includes all content, not just the documents in their document repositories or a knowledge base somewhere on their intranet, but all documents, including paper and electronic.

Because of this push, the ECM business is growing rapidly in the Information Technology sector, and vendors are rapidly ramping up their offerings. This can make choosing the best platform a constant challenge. The interesting part of this new growth is that it involves some older technologies and processes that were available before the current global regulatory situation changed.

For example, despite being in usage for approximately 30 years, imaging still continues to provide strong return on investment. Many futurists predicted that imaging would fade away, replaced by online signature capture systems and digital libraries. Surprisingly, imaging systems have stood the test of time and withstood the scrutiny of the legal system. Since companies still use paper and paper is still unmanageable on a large scale, companies continue to need imaging systems to manage the flow of paper documents within their organizations, in addition to management of digitally created documents.

Business leaders and project managers should shift their organization's approach for managing unstructured content away from focusing solely on electronically created documents and Web content management solutions to an integrated ECM direction. Whatever solution the company chooses should include a phased-in approach that clearly defines each phase's components, deliverables, and expected savings. Spread the costs of the biggest system components over a group of departments large enough to allow the expense to be absorbed slowly into the enterprise, while demonstrating a healthy ROI.

To accomplish this, it is important that the ECM project managers work with business process owners to communicate how an ECM approach provides economic benefits, such as more accountability, better risk management, and lower overall operations costs. ECM project managers should also develop a conservative, well-documented strategy for ensuring continuous improvement of the business processes involved. Developing a thorough business case not only demonstrates the costs versus the benefits of ECM but also highlights where a company needs to improve as a business. ECM is not easy, it is complex; but in the right hands, it can deliver tremendous business benefits.

Although FileNet is not the end-all solution in enterprise content management, it is a major player with a strongly entrenched customer base and a continuously evolving product line. If an organization is looking for an experienced market leader in this field with the bench strength to continue delivering value for decades, it can look to FileNet.

Success Story

In 1996, analysts noticed large differences among regional hospitals in the success rate for heart surgery. In response, teams of highly experienced heart surgeons from five major medical centers observed each other's operating-room practices. Next, they conducted a dialog about their most effective techniques and policies. The results were documented and distributed, which led to more dialog and more document distributions.

The result was an astounding 24% drop in the overall mortality rate for coronary bypass surgery. This was not a savings of projected soft dollars but the confirmed saving of 74 lives. Surely, saving lives represents the ultimate return-on-investment, and the key tool required was simple collaboration.

This success story did not involve a FileNet implementation, but it does show how data analysis, documentation, and dialog enable groups to find new collaboration opportunities, examine potential process improvements, and recognize best practices to share.

Seeking to use computing as a tool to simplify the storage and organization of business records is an important goal. However, the ease with which digitally created objects can be controlled will never alone provide sufficient value to justify the loss of flexibility that comes from giving up use of paper documents.

Study the paper documents and their workflows within your company before you attempt to eliminate them. For centuries, the sharing of information most often occurred verbally through myths, legends, and stories. Printing technology improved the process in many ways, but it never eliminated its predecessors. Directing the evolving role of documents within an organization requires studying *both* the history and the future of knowledge sharing.

INDEX